IRISH HISTORY

THE NORMANS

DEADLY! IRISH HISTORY – THE VIKINGS
'Madcap, marauding, entertaining and highly informative … full of facts, legends and stories about Viking life. There are cartoons and comics; tongue-in-cheek 'newspaper articles', 'documents' and 'catalogues' … all proving that Irish history isn't boring at all … it's deadly!' More Deadly! Irish History, please!'

Fallen Star Stories

DEADLY! IRISH HISTORY – THE CELTS
'Accessible, anarchic and crammed with cartoons and wacky illustrations, this book is as deadly as Irish history gets!'

RTÉ Guide

'Farrelly's writing and drawings never miss a beat in this well-informed and witty account of the Celts … with comic strips, guess-the-answer sessions, roll-the-dice-to-see-which-character-you-are games, how to make your own games board or roundhouse … Great fun!'

Children's Books Ireland

John Farrelly was born and raised in a village just outside Newry, Co. Down. He wouldn't say the house he lived in as a child was dirty but even the mice wore overalls. His father was a parachutist who he always looked up to. At school, his worst subject was maths. If he had 10 pennies for every bad maths exam he did, he'd have 73 pennies. After flunking art college, he got a job playing the triangle in an orchestra. He quit because it was just one ting after another. Everybody laughed at him when he said he'd write funny books one day. They're not laughing now. This is the third book in the **DEADLY! IRISH HISTORY** series.

You'll see **Deadly! Data Cards** every so often throughout this book that feature some of Ireland's most famous castles. Each card gives a brief rundown of the castle's history including the century when a castle or fortified dwelling was *first* built on the site and most importantly whether it is haunted! **WOOOOO!** Unfortunately, because there are so many castles in Ireland and this is just a wee little book, I couldn't show them all and had to leave out any that were built in later centuries. Therefore your personal favourite might not be mentioned, so I'm really, very sorry. And I'm not just saying that.

DEADLY! IRISH HISTORY

THE NORMANS

WRITTEN AND ILLUSTRATED BY
JOHN FARRELLY

THE O'BRIEN PRESS
DUBLIN

Dedication

For Garry, who's been watching my back since we were eleven.
You'd think he'd be bored by now.

Acknowledgements

Thank you to Dervilia Roche for her help in obtaining reference material. Thanks again to Dr Matthew C. Stout for his historical knowledge and Conor Fearon for his Irish language skills. Thanks to Bex Sheridan for her design prowess and endless patience. And thank you to my editor Susan Houlden for making me say 'tsk' every time she got me to change something. She was usually right!

First published 2022 by The O'Brien Press Ltd,
12 Terenure Road East, Rathgar, Dublin 6, D06 HD27, Ireland.
Tel: +353 1 4923333; Fax: +353 1 4922777
E-mail: books@obrien.ie
Website: obrien.ie
The O'Brien Press is a member of Publishing Ireland.
ISBN: 978-1-78849-287-4

Copyright for text and illustrations © John Farrelly
The moral rights of the author have been asserted.
Cover design: Emma Byrne
Internal design: Bex Sheridan
Copyright for typesetting, layout, editing, design
© The O'Brien Press Ltd

All rights reserved. No part of this publication may be reproduced or utilised in any form or by any means, electronic or mechanical, including photocopying, recording or in any information storage and retrieval system, without permission in writing from the publisher.

1 3 5 7 6 4 2
22 24 26 25 23

Printed in the UK by Clays Ltd, Elcograf S.p.A.
The paper in this book is produced using pulp from managed forests

Published in
DUBLIN
UNESCO
City of Literature

Growing up with
O'BRIEN
obrien.ie

CONTENTS

Introduction	6
It's the Fort That Counts – Before Castles	10
Naughty Normans – Strongbow and the Norman Invasion	13
We Moat Be Here For a While – Building a Castle	22
An Irishman's (Tower) House is His Castle – Tower Houses	36
You're Not Going Out in That! – Medieval Fashion	42
Odd Jobs – Work and Trade	49
This One Will Slay You – War and Fighting	58
Medieval and Medigood – Crime and Punishment	74
You Want Me To Eat What?!? – Food and Drink	82
Bleeding Good Humour – Medieval Medicine	90
Winding Down – Fun and Leisure	100
Isobel, Hugh and Fionntán – Medieval Kids	109
Séamus the Sinister Swordsman	120
Visiting a Castle Ruin	132
Normans' Land – Legacy of the Normans	134
Famous Irish Castles Map	138
Timeline	139
Answers	142

INTRODUCTION

You can't go far in Ireland without bumping into a flippin' castle. They're *everywhere!* There were hundreds of castles of all shapes and sizes in Ireland. Because most of them are now in ruins, you'd be forgiven for thinking they're really ancient but they only started springing up in the late 12th century. That's just a dozen of your granda's lifetimes ago (or two dozen of your dad's lifetimes. Or seventy of yours. Or three hundred and forty of your pet hamster's).

The word castle comes from the Latin word *castellum* meaning 'fortified place' and although there were strong stone structures built by the native Irish many centuries ago, these couldn't be called 'castles' in the way we know them today. When we picture a castle we think of big, thick walls, battlements, towers, moats and drawbridges. Many, but not all, castles had these things. Historians mostly agree that for a castle to be a castle, it not only had to be fortified, it also had to be lived in by royalty or nobility.

The nobles who lived in these castles were people from another land who came to Ireland, liked what they saw and decided they wanted to stay. More and more of them came, throwing their weight around like school-yard bullies and building castles all over the place. But how did the Irish just allow this to happen, you might say? Hadn't they learnt their lesson from just a few hundred years before when the Vikings did the same thing?* This time it was different. It's said that a vampire cannot enter a house unless he is invited in and that's exactly what happened here – the invaders, like vampires, were invited into Ireland.

* See *Deadly! Irish History – The Vikings*.

But *who* were these invaders? *Why* did they build so many castles? *Where* did they come from? And most importantly, *what eejit invited them*? Well, that's why we're here – to find out the answers to all these **DEADLY!** questions and so much more. Like how these people lived, what they wore, the jobs they did, the food they ate and whether they were *all* bad. But first, let's have a look at what came before castles ...

IT'S THE FORT THAT COUNTS

BEFORE CASTLES

There were plenty of fortified structures that were built in Ireland before the invaders arrived.

PROMONTORY FORTS were stone forts built upon the steep cliffs of Ireland's coastlines, probably as a refuge from invaders and as a good spot to keep watch. They date back to the Iron Age.

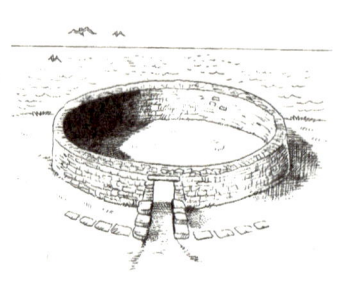

RINGFORTS were circular settlements with a protective ditch and wooden walls, home for many Irish people between the 5th and 10th centuries.

CASHELS were stone ringforts that were built mostly in the west of Ireland.

CRANNÓGS were fortified dwellings built on an artifical island in a river or lake.

LONGPHUIRT were forts built by the Vikings for protection from the local Irish.

ROUND TOWERS were tall circular towers usually built near monasteries. They date to around the 10th and 11th centuries when monasteries were under attack from both Viking and Irish raiders.

MOTTE-AND-BAILEY CASTLES were temporary fortresses built by invaders. They took only a few weeks to build and consisted of a mound called a motte with a wooden structure called a keep on top. A noble and his family could live in this. At the foot of the mound was an enclosure called a bailey where the noble's men lived.

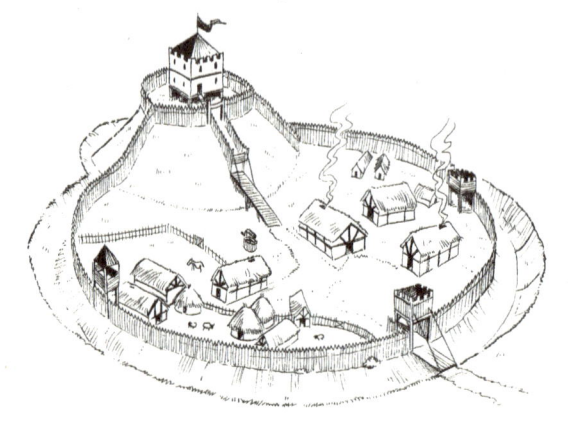

STONE CASTLES were sometimes built on the sites of motte-and-bailey castles. MUCH more on these later!

NAUGHTY NORMANS
STRONGBOW AND THE NORMAN INVASION

Remember the Vikings? Those wild, adventuring warriors who pillaged Ireland in the 8th century and ended up staying? Well, in the year 911, some Vikings led by a fella called Rollo killed, looted and burned their way through France, so much so that the French king, a guy called Charles the Simple, ended up giving them lands in northern France to make them stop. A bit like when your ma gives your wee brother a lolly in the supermarket to stop him from throwing a tantrum.

These Vikings settled down like they did in Ireland and married into noble French families. Everyone called them 'Northmen' (because they came from way up north in Scandinavia and now lived in the north of France) or 'Normans' and the area they lived in became known as Normandy.

The Normans, having the same adventurous spirit as their Viking ancestors, soon set their sights on England, and the Norman King William defeated the Saxon (English) King Harold at the famous Battle of Hastings in 1066. The tale of the battle was turned into an embroidered cloth around 70 metres long and 50 centimetres tall, now called The Bayeux Tapestry – a bit like a comic strip.

The Normans made themselves at home. They built castles everywhere (over eighty in just seventeen years), marrying into noble English families (becoming 'Anglo-Norman') and into Welsh families ('Cambro-Norman'). In this book, we'll just call them Normans. It wasn't long before they came knocking on Ireland's door. But who invited them in?

The story goes that a lady called Dervorgilla (in Irish Derbfhorgaill, pronounced *Derv-or-gill*), who was the wife of Tiernan O'Rourke (Tigernán Ua Ruairc, *Tear-nauwn Ooh-a Rork*), the brutal king of Breifne, was kidnapped by his arch-nemesis, Diarmuid MacMurrough (Diarmait Mac Murchada, *Deer-mid Mack Mwer-chah-dah*), the king of Leinster, in the year 1152. Another story says that she wanted to go because she hated her husband.

After Tiernan found out, he went to the High King of Ireland, Rory O'Connor (Ruaidrí Ua Conchobair, *Roar-ee Ooh-a Kohn-ko-var*), and he took the kingdom of Leinster away from Diarmuid as punishment for abducting Dervorgilla, even though it was fourteen years after the event! Diarmuid fled across the water to England and France to ask the English King, Henry II, for help getting his kingdom back. Henry allowed Diarmuid to borrow some of his soldiers. Diarmuid returned to Ireland and, with the help of Henry's soldiers and a Norman knight called Richard de Clare (also known by the nickname *Strongbow*), he took his kingdom back.

This is Richard 'Strongbow' de Clare, Earl of Pembroke – a Norman knight from Wales. He is a rather tall lad, is Strongbow! Which of his statements are straight as an arrow and which have missed their mark? **Answers below.**

A) DIARMUID MACMURROUGH PROMISED ME HIS DAUGHTER AOIFE'S HAND IN MARRIAGE IF I HELPED HIM WIN BACK HIS KINGDOM.

B) I GOT MY NICKNAME BECAUSE OF HOW GREAT I AM WITH A BOW AND ARROW.

C) I CAME TO IRELAND FOR THE FIRST TIME IN 1170 WITH 100 KNIGHTS AND 500 FOOT SOLDIERS.

D) KING HENRY II CAME TO IRELAND IN 1171 BECAUSE HE WAS AFRAID I WAS GETTING TOO STRONG AND POWERFUL.

ANSWERS: Strongbow lied twice. a) True. Diarmuid gave Strongbow his daughter and therefore the kingdom of Leinster when Diarmuid died. b) Nah – he probably got his nickname from a mistranslation of a word which means 'Foreign Pants'. c) No. Strongbow came with 200 knights and 1,500 foot soldiers who were very well armed. They landed in Wexford and defeated the poorly equipped Irish armies at Wexford, Waterford and Dublin. d) Yup. After Strongbow gained all Diarmuid's land and wealth when Diarmuid died in 1171, Henry decided to pay Strongbow a visit.

If the details about the Norman invasion sound a little confusing, here's a bit of a sing-song to help explain it better.

DEADLY! IRISH HISTORY presents THRONE AWAY — The Saga of Dervorgilla and Diarmuid

♪ YOU CAN CALL ME *DERVORGILLA*, A FAIR AND LOVELY LADY.
I'M MARRIED TO KING TIERNAN OF WHOM I'M A BIT AFRAIDY!
MY BROTHER'S HATCHED A PLAN TO HELP ME ESCAPE HIS CLUTCHES
BUT IF MY HUSBAND SMELLS A RAT, HE'LL PUT US BOTH *IN CRUTCHES*! ♪

♪ HOWAYA – I'M *DIARMUID* OF LEINSTER I'M THE KING
AND TO MY FORTRESS DOWN AT FERNS, DERVORGILLA I WILL BRING!
I AIN'T SCARED OF TIERNAN – IN FACT I THINK HE'S *CHICKEN*
SO IF HE COMES LOOKIN' FOR HIS MISSUS I'LL GIVE HIM *SUCH A KICKIN'*! ♪

♪ I'M TIERNAN, KING OF BREIFNE AND BY MY VERY LIFE,
I'M GONNA GET THE KING OF IRELAND TO HELP ME *FIND MY WIFE*!
AND WHEN SHE'S BACK WITH ME I'LL ASK HER, NO MISTAKIN',
"DID YA GO WITH DIARMUID WILLINGLY OR WERE YA *FLIPPIN' TAKEN*?!" ♪

ALL HAIL RORY, KING OF IRELAND - BY GOLLY THAT IS ME! I'LL HELP POOR TIERNAN FIND HIS WIFE AND DO IT HAPPILY! OUR ARMIES WILL JOIN FORCES AND I SWEAR ON MY ROYAL BEARD WHEN DIARMUID SEES US COMING HE'LL SURELY BE AFEARED!
DERVORGILLA'S BACK WITH CRUEL TIERNAN AND NOW I'VE LOST MY LAND SO I SAILED AWAY OVERSEAS TO ASK KING HENRY FOR A HAND! HE'S LENT ME SOLDIERS, KNIGHTS AND MERCENARIES, ALL ARE GOOD TO GO PLUS A RATHER TALL AND FRECKLED LAD WHO CALLS HIMSELF STRONGBOW!
OOH YEAH, I AM STRONGBOW - YOU'VE LIKELY HEARD OF ME! MINE'S A NAME THAT WILL LIVE FOREVER DOWN THROUGH IRISH HISTORY!
AND THOUGH ALL US NORMANS ORIGINALLY CAME FROM FRANCE, WHEN I WAS OFFERED AN IRISH KINGDOM, I JUMPED RIGHT AT THE CHANCE!

BRINGING STRONGBOW AND THE NORMANS HERE, THAT'S MY *AWFUL SIN!* BLAME ME, IT'S ALL MY FAULT, 'TWAS *ME* INVITED THEM IN! BUT *ASK* YOURSELF THIS QUESTION PLEASE, IF YOU DO ONE THING THIS DAY: WOULD THE NORMANS HAVE INVADED IRELAND SOME TIME *ANYWAY?*
THIS IS THE *QUESTION* ... THE QUESTION WE SHOULD ASK MAYBE ... *MAYBE* THE PERSON WE SHOULD BRING TO TASK ...
IS SOMEONE ... *SOMEONE* POWERFUL WHO LIVES WAY DOWN IN ROME ...
THE ENGLISHMAN CALLED ADRIAN WHO SITS ON THE PAPAL THRONE!
HURRAH!
CLAP! CLAP!
BRAVO!
MORE! MORE!
ENCORE!

What's an English pope got to do with it? Well, Pope Adrian IV (real name, Nicholas Breakspear – the only English pope, *ever*) issued a Papal Bull (an official order) giving King Henry II permission to invade Ireland ...

... FOR THE CORRECTION OF MORALS AND THE INTRODUCTION OF VIRTUES AND FOR THE ADVANCEMENT OF THE CHRISTIAN RELIGION.

Adrian also ordered every home in Ireland to pay a new tax that would go to Rome. This was in 1156, more than a decade before any Norman set foot in Ireland. But Henry was so busy fighting elsewhere that invading Ireland wasn't high on his list of priorities, at least until Diarmuid MacMurrough came looking for his help. It was only late in 1171 that Henry sailed to Ireland himself when he heard Strongbow was getting too big for his boots, but the blame for the invasion of Ireland could be laid squarely at the feet of Pope Adrian IV, not Diarmuid MacMurrough or Dervorgilla.*

---

* Dervorgilla went on to outlive Tiernan, Diarmuid, Rory, Strongbow and Pope Adrian and died at the ripe old age of eighty-five.

Once the door was opened to the Normans, there was no stopping them. Supported by the Church in Rome, the invasion of Ireland spread. The towns that had been established by the Vikings – Dublin, Waterford, Wexford, Cork and Limerick – became crown land, meaning King Henry II declared them to be his. The Irish had failed to unite against the Vikings and, once again, they failed to join forces against the new invaders. Most of the Irish kings submitted to King Henry.

Henry gave the entire kingdom of Meath to a knight called Hugh de Lacy, and even though Henry signed a treaty (agreement) with Irish High King Rory O'Connor (Ruaidrí Ua Conchobair) in 1175 promising he wouldn't take any more land, the Normans continued to invade.

The Normans also had better weapons and training than the Irish, and there was one other key thing that helped them invade: the building of their mighty castles.

Hugh de Lacy

WE MOAT BE HERE FOR A WHILE

BUILDING A CASTLE

The Normans lost no time in building wooden forts in strategic locations. These took quite a short time to build (maybe a few weeks) and were called motte-and-bailey castles.

After a few years, they built stone castles, like in France and England. It could take up to twenty years and millions in today's money to build one. It also cost a lot to keep it running with workers cooking, cleaning, making things and doing repairs, as well as soldiers to defend the castle against attackers.

A DEADLY! GUIDE TO ...
BUILDING A CASTLE

1) Choose a good spot to build your castle. Pick a spot with a great view of the surrounding countryside. It needs to be close to a supply of water, timber and stone. You need a solid foundation to take the weight of thick stone walls. Some castles are built on a hill, a cliff or an island. This makes your castle easier to defend, and it can be seen for miles around. You are a rich, powerful, important person and you want people to know it.

2) The master mason — the guy in charge of building your castle — makes a wooden model first. You can move bits around until you decide on the design.

3) Your master mason hires a team of stonemasons (skilled workers) and roughmasons (less-skilled workers) to cut and shape the stone for the walls. A mason gets paid for every stone he shapes into *ashlar* – flat-surfaced blocks – so the quicker they work, the more they get paid. Each mason chips a special mark into the stone so the master mason knows how much to pay him.

Masonry tools

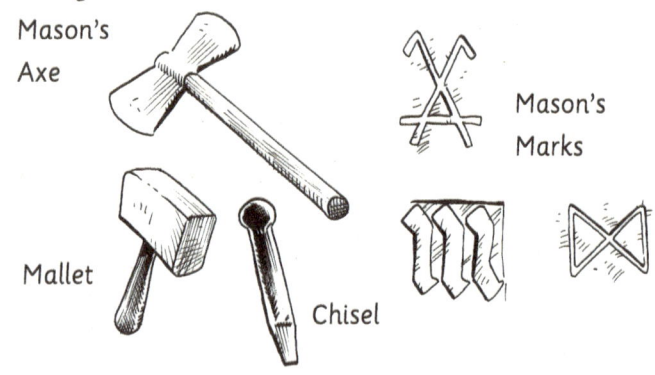

Mason's Axe

Mason's Marks

Mallet

Chisel

4) A man operates a crane by walking around in a treadmill. Loads as heavy as 500 kg could be lifted this way.

5) Carpenters make scaffolding for the builders and they also shape timbers for the ceilings and towers. Blacksmiths make tools, chains, hinges and nails (you need thousands of nails) and general labourers make mortar (by heating chalk or limestone) and do all the donkey work. Pulleys and ropes are used to lift buckets and heavy wooden beams.

Carpentry tools

Gimlet   Brace   Axe   Adze   Saw

6) The main walls are packed with rubble mixed with mortar. Some castle walls can be up to 5 metres thick. They are built like this to withstand attack.

7) The keep is the part of the castle where you will live and spend most of your time. It is fitted out with a great hall, kitchens, chapel, bedchambers, latrine towers (toilets) and, of course, a dungeon.

8) Make sure the defences are installed – a moat, drawbridge and portcullis are essential, not to mention fashionable – for a noble like you. Just because it is only Normans who live in castles doesn't mean you all like each other, so your castle is sure to be attacked sooner or later. Also, the local Irish population aren't too fond of you either. Not that you care.

9) When it's finished, have your castle painted with a white lime wash so it almost seems to shine brightly.* Now you can move in and enjoy your new home. Don't forget to stock up on food and supplies in case there's a siege!

* Some castles in Ireland may have been painted with a yellow, orange or pink lime wash

INSIDE A CASTLE

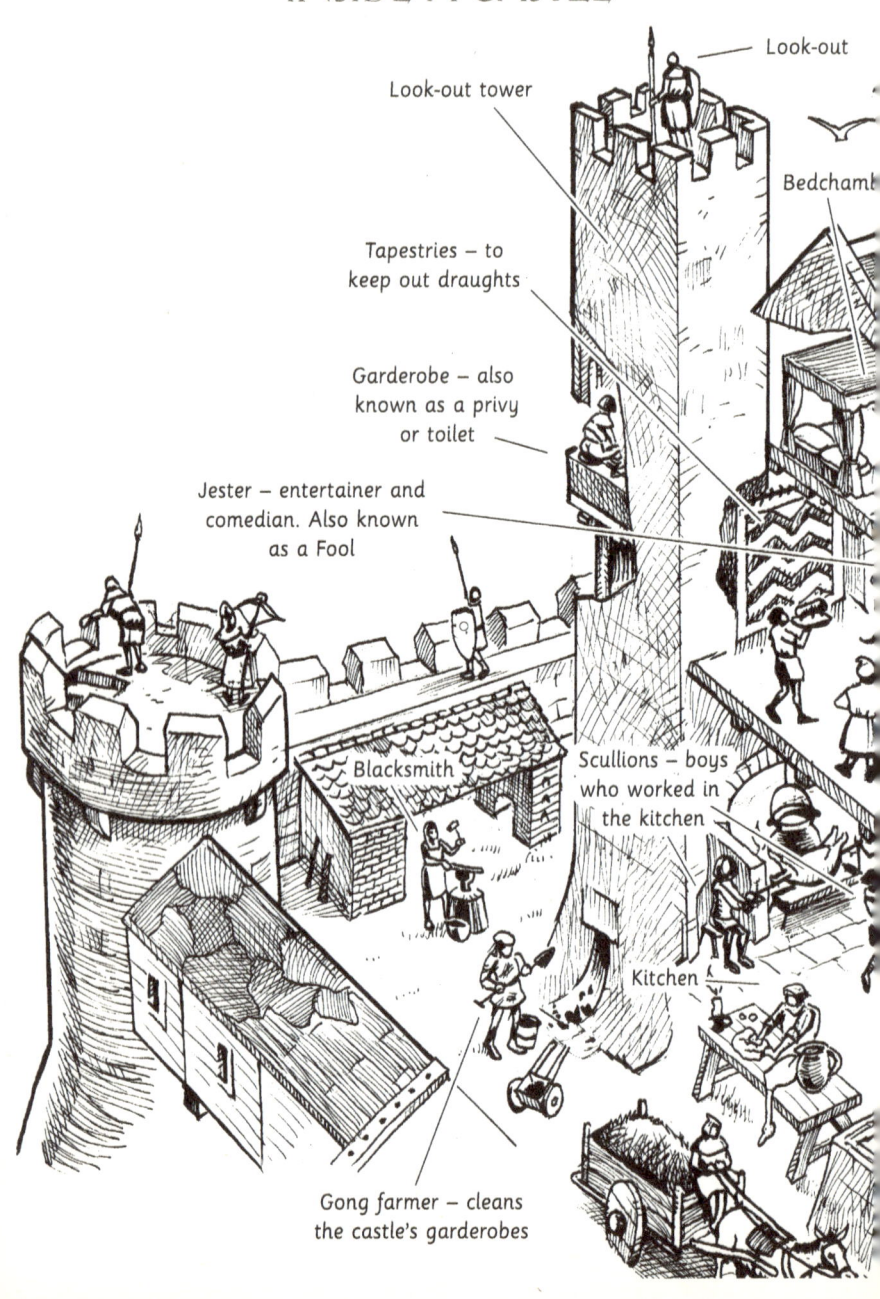

Look-out

Look-out tower

Bedchamber

Tapestries – to keep out draughts

Garderobe – also known as a privy or toilet

Jester – entertainer and comedian. Also known as a Fool

Blacksmith

Scullions – boys who worked in the kitchen

Kitchen

Gong farmer – cleans the castle's garderobes

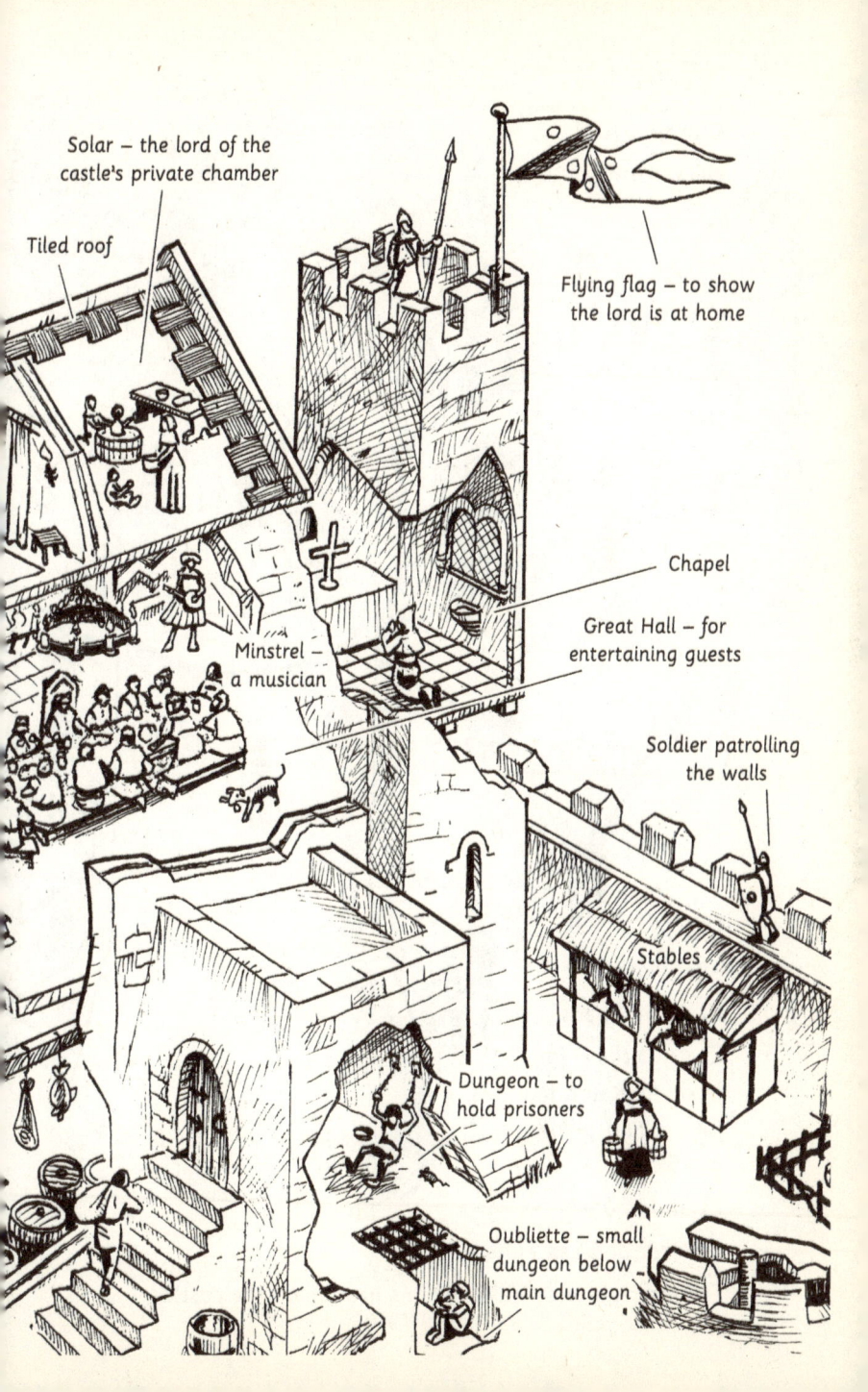

- Solar – the lord of the castle's private chamber
- Tiled roof
- Flying flag – to show the lord is at home
- Chapel
- Great Hall – for entertaining guests
- Minstrel – a musician
- Soldier patrolling the walls
- Stables
- Dungeon – to hold prisoners
- Oubliette – small dungeon below main dungeon

DEADLY! MEDLEY

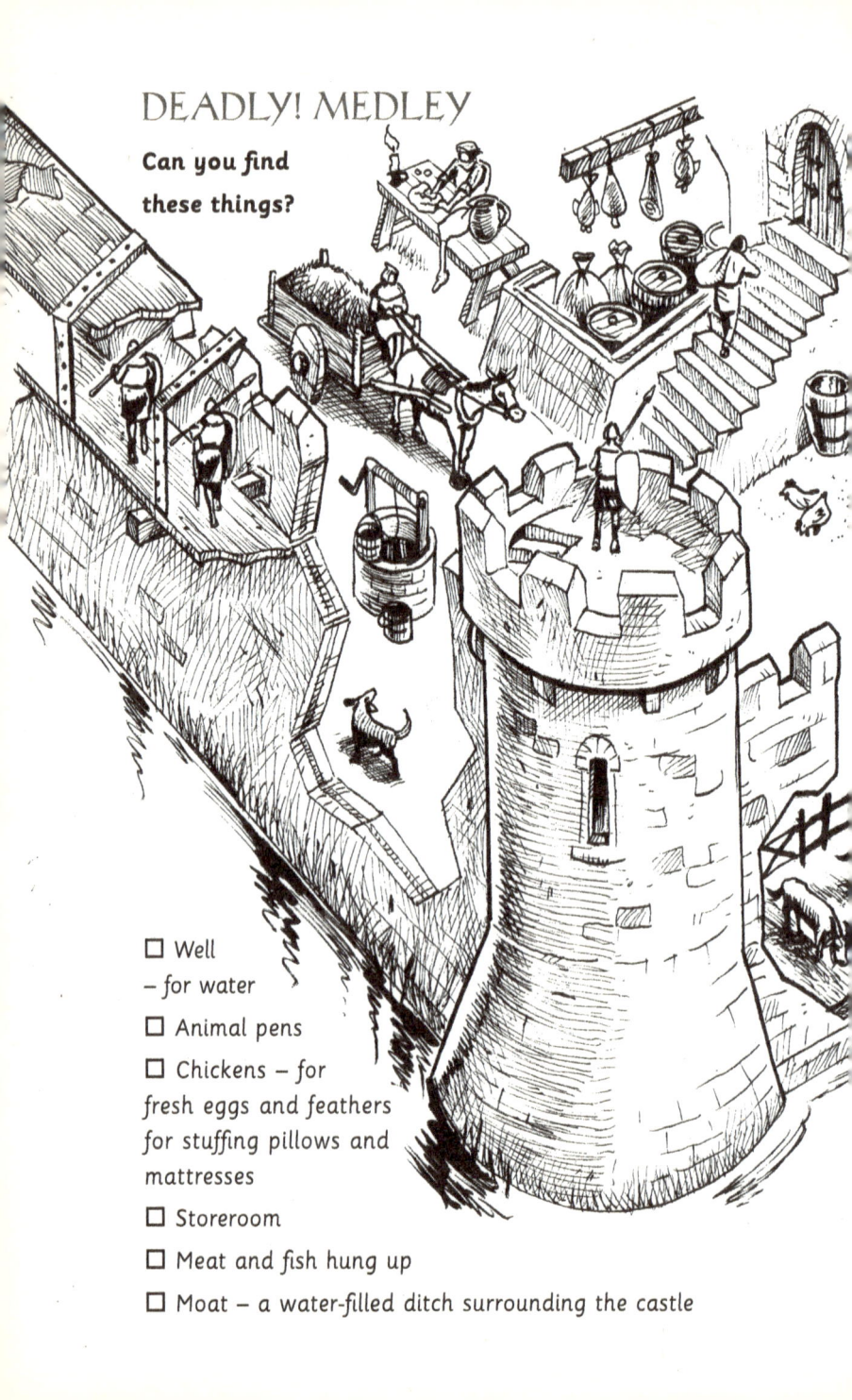

Can you find these things?

☐ Well
– for water
☐ Animal pens
☐ Chickens – for fresh eggs and feathers for stuffing pillows and mattresses
☐ Storeroom
☐ Meat and fish hung up
☐ Moat – a water-filled ditch surrounding the castle

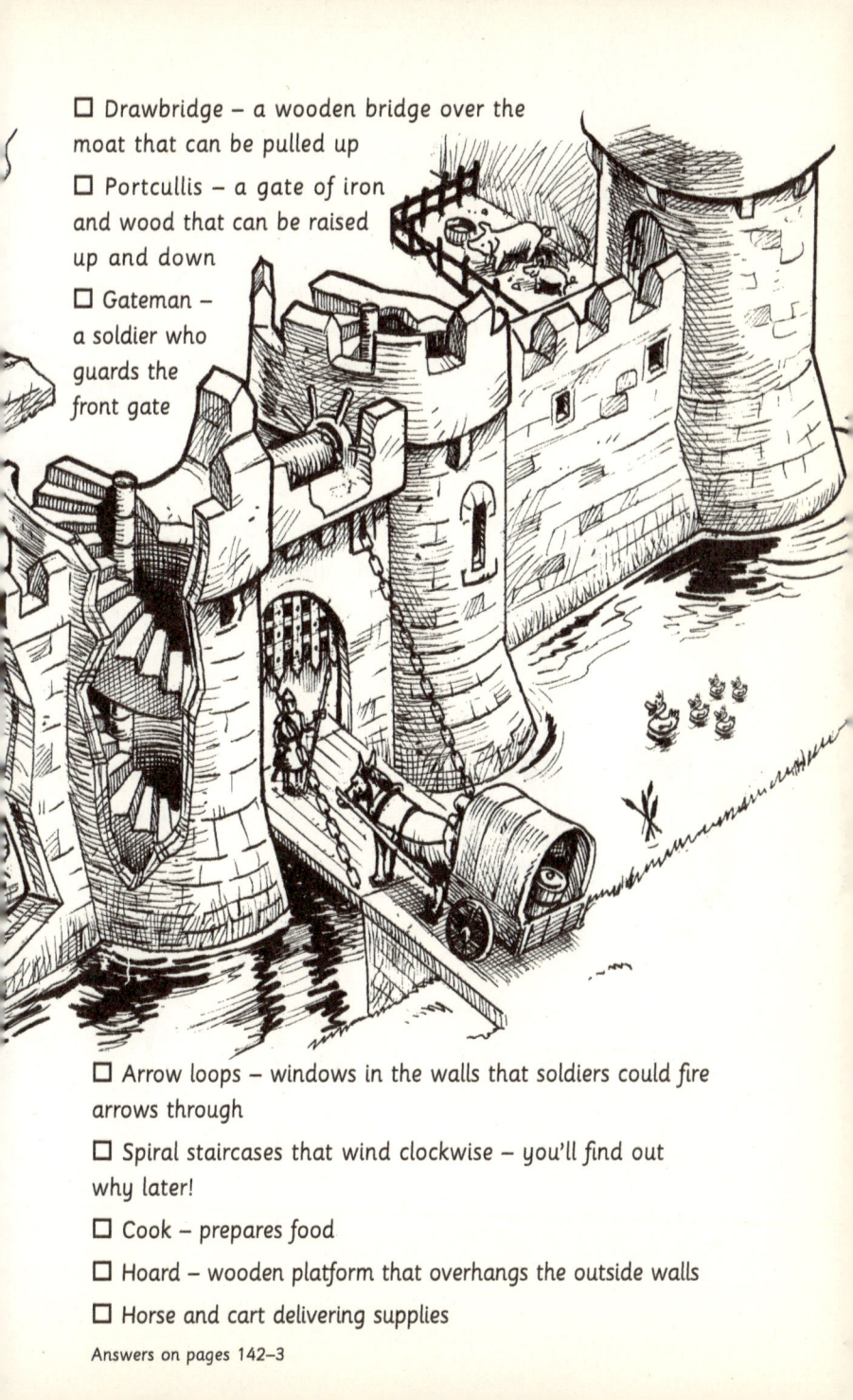

☐ Drawbridge – a wooden bridge over the moat that can be pulled up

☐ Portcullis – a gate of iron and wood that can be raised up and down

☐ Gateman – a soldier who guards the front gate

☐ Arrow loops – windows in the walls that soldiers could fire arrows through

☐ Spiral staircases that wind clockwise – you'll find out why later!

☐ Cook – prepares food

☐ Hoard – wooden platform that overhangs the outside walls

☐ Horse and cart delivering supplies

Answers on pages 142–3

MAKE YOUR OWN CASTLE

1) Cut 4 pieces of cardboard (each 22 cm x 16 cm). Draw a battlement pattern on them to make your castle walls.

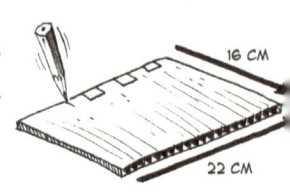

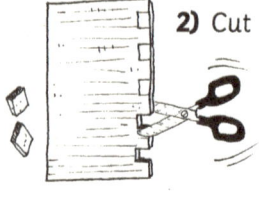

2) Cut out the battlements.

3) Draw a battlement pattern on four kitchen roll tubes (or two toilet roll tubes taped together) and cut those out. These are the castle's towers.

4) Cut a slit up the side of each tube the same height as the castle wall. Rotate the tube 90° and cut another slit.

5) Draw a gateway on one of the walls and cut it out. Keep the piece you cut out to use as your castle's drawbridge.

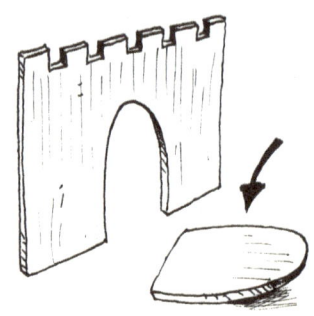

6) Cut a piece of cardboard 40 cm x 40 cm for the castle's base. Use one of the walls to measure out a square in the centre. Draw a moat around that.

7) Paint the square grey, the moat blue and the grass green. You can glue down shiny blue gift wrap for the moat instead.

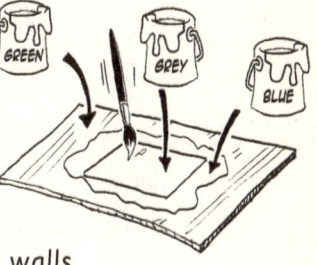

8) Paint the walls and towers grey or whatever colour you want – castles were painted with different colours to make them stand out more.

9) Paint the drawbridge brown and add lines with a black marker.

10) Draw arrow loops on the walls and add a brick pattern.

BRICK PATTERN

11) Make two holes near the top of the drawbridge with a sharp pencil. Then make two holes either side of the gateway. (You might need an adult's help with this.)

12) Cut two pieces of string the same length and tie a paper fastener to each of the ends.

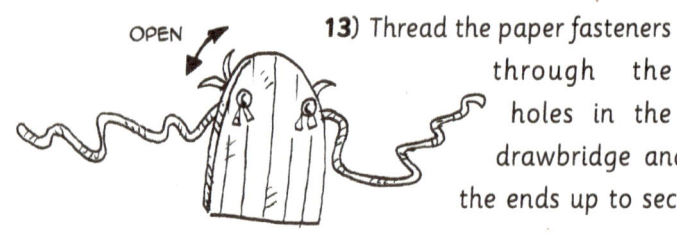

13) Thread the paper fasteners through the holes in the drawbridge and open the ends up to secure.

14) Tape the walls together with masking tape.

15) Tape the walls to the base then slot the towers into each of the corners.

16) Thread the string through the holes either side of the gateway and tape the drawbridge where shown to make a 'hinge'.

17) Make flags using toothpicks and triangular pieces of coloured paper. Tape these to the inside of each of the towers.

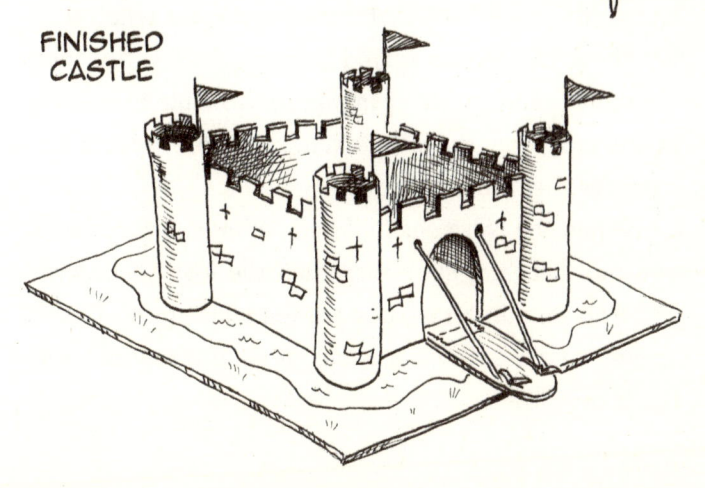

FINISHED CASTLE

AN IRISHMAN'S (TOWER) HOUSE IS HIS CASTLE

TOWER HOUSES

The Normans and their descendants suddenly stopped building castles around the year 1348, when a terrible disease called the Black Death hit Ireland and wiped out many thousands of people. (More on this later.) When the Irish kings and chieftains – who had been living the traditional Irish way in ringforts, crannógs and cashels – saw how good the Norman castles were at withstanding attack, they wanted to get in on the act of building their own. These were a bit different from the Norman design of castle and became known as tower houses. Historians debate whether or not these can be considered 'proper' castles, but there are many, many more examples of this style of building in Ireland than the other kind, so most people just consider them to be castles.

When the Normans had been in Ireland for a while and had become 'more Irish than the Irish themselves' (Hiberno-Norman), they also started building this style of smaller castle. Let's have a look at what a typical tower house was like ...

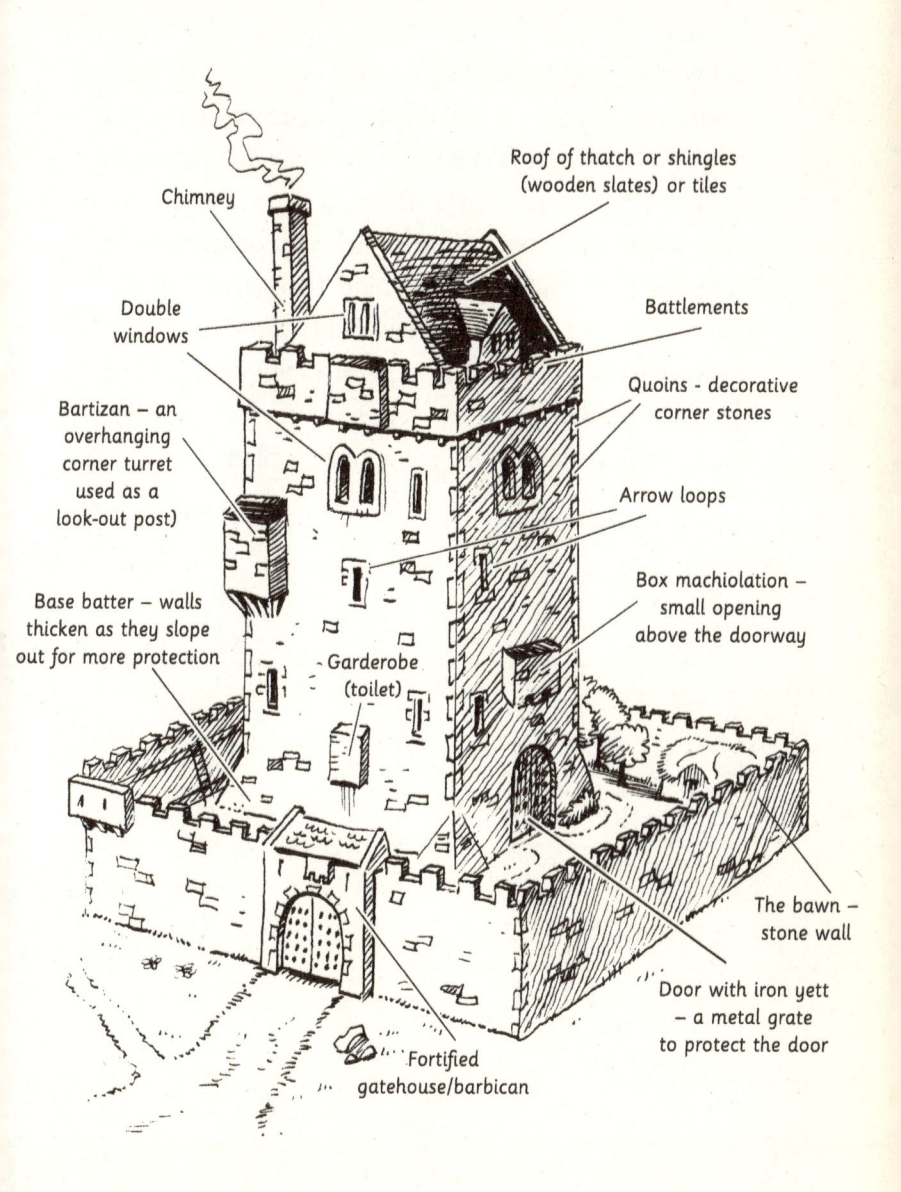

- Chimney
- Roof of thatch or shingles (wooden slates) or tiles
- Double windows
- Battlements
- Bartizan – an overhanging corner turret used as a look-out post)
- Quoins – decorative corner stones
- Arrow loops
- Base batter – walls thicken as they slope out for more protection
- Box machiolation – small opening above the doorway
- Garderobe (toilet)
- The bawn – stone wall
- Fortified gatehouse/barbican
- Door with iron yett – a metal grate to protect the door

At the end of the 16th century, both English and Irish nobility started building fortified houses. These were usually rectangular or L-shaped, three-storey buildings with high gables, large chimneys and big windows. Some of them had square towers at the corners. Sometimes, tower houses had extra features like square towers and bartizans built onto them, turning them into fortified houses. Fortified houses were usually surrounded by a bawn which had towers, heavily protected gateways and gunloops (similar to arrow loops in Norman castles). These fortified houses also came to be called castles.

This is Gerald of Wales. After he made a couple of visits to Ireland in the 1180s, he wrote two books about Ireland and its people. With him being a Norman, not everything he wrote about the Irish was tickety-boo. Did he really write these things in his books? **Answers below.**

A) I MET TWO WEREWOLVES IN IRELAND.

B) THE IRISH INVENTED MUSIC BUT THE SCOTS AND THE WELSH ARE BETTER AT IT.

C) THE IRISH PEOPLE ARE LAZY, WILD AND BARBARIC.

D) THE IRISH ARE A BUNCH OF LIARS.

ANSWERS: Gerald actually wrote all of these things about the Irish and more, probably because he wanted them to look bad. It worked. People believed his tales for years to come. a) He wrote that he met two werewolves (called *The Werewolves of Ossory*) even though he had copied the story from an older one. b) Gerald said that the Irish people invented music but could only play two instruments while the Scots and Welsh played three. c) Gerald loved to bad-mouth the Irish as much as he could. d) He's one to talk.

FAMOUS IRISH CASTLES #1*

CASTLE ROCHE CO. LOUTH
12

CENTURY FIRST BUILT: 12TH
HAUNTED: 🏵
DEADLINESS: 7

This unusual triangular-shaped castle is the only castle in Ireland known to have been built by a woman, Rohesia de Verdun. Legend says Rohesia threw the architect who designed the castle to his death from an upstairs window. Some people say they've seen the ghost of a falling man at the site.

CARLINGFORD CASTLE CO. LOUTH
9

CENTURY BUILT: 12TH
HAUNTED: 🏵🏵
DEADLINESS: 6

This castle was built on the shores of Carlingford Lough by the Norman baron Hugh de Lacy. The ghost of Henrietta Travescant, The Black Abbess, is often seen walking amongst the ruins. The castle sits in the shadow of Slieve Foy, the mountain where legendary warrior Fionn Mac Cumhaill is said to be buried.

KILKENNY CASTLE CO. KILKENNY
29

CENTURY BUILT: 12TH
HAUNTED: 🏵
DEADLINESS: 7

Kilkenny castle was built by none other than Strongbow himself. It was home to the powerful Butler family of Ormond, the ancient region of East Munster, for nearly 600 years. The castle's dungeon is said to be haunted by the ghost of a servant boy who died there in the 17th century. On cold, wintry nights you may hear the sound of him weeping.

NARROW WATER CASTLE CO. DOWN
33

CENTURY FIRST BUILT: 12TH
HAUNTED: 🏵🏵
DEADLINESS: 7

The first castle built here belonged to the Norman baron Hugh de Lacy, but the existing building dates from the 16th century when the castle guarded Carlingford Lough. The castle was owned for a short time by Chief of the Mournes, Hugh Magennis, before being recaptured by the English. Lassara Magennis threw herself off the top of the castle and drowned after her musician boyfriend was killed on the night they were running away to be married. Eerie harp music can sometimes be heard while the sad ghost of Lassara floats down from the top of the castle.

KILLBRITTAIN CASTLE CO. CORK

27

CENTURY BUILT: 11TH
HAUNTED: 0
DEADLINESS: 5

The original castle on this site was built in 1035 by Brian Boru's grandson, Cian, and is one of the first ever castles to be built in Ireland. It was once home to Russell Winn, the inventor of the bomb-disposal robot and is the oldest continuously inhabited castle in Ireland.

DUNLUCE CASTLE CO. ANTRIM

19

CENTURY BUILT: 14TH
HAUNTED: 🎃🎃🎃
DEADLINESS: 9

This breathtaking castle was built upon cliffs overlooking the ocean. Many people have fallen to their deaths on the rocks far below. The ghost of a woman called Maeve Roe is said to haunt the castle, with people hearing her cries on stormy nights. Also, an English soldier who was hanged there haunts one of the towers.

NEWTOWN CASTLE CO. CLARE

34

CENTURY BUILT: 16TH
HAUNTED: 0
DEADLINESS: 5

Built by the powerful O'Brien clan, this castle is one of only a few cylindrical tower houses in Ireland. It also has an unusual square pyramid base. A man called Charles O'Loughlin, who called himself King of the Burren, once lived here.

FOULKSRATH CASTLE CO. KILKENNY

23

CENTURY BUILT: 14TH
HAUNTED: 🎃🎃🎃
DEADLINESS: 8

This tower house is home to three ghosts, one of whom was a guard who fell asleep on lookout duty and was thrown off the roof as punishment. A relative of Jonathan Swift, who wrote *Gulliver's Travels*, made the first Irish aeroplane here in 1872. Using his butler as the pilot, he launched it with a giant catapult off the top of the castle, where it immediately plunged to the ground. Luckily the butler survived but with many broken bones!

* See map, page 138.

YOU'RE NOT GOING OUT IN THAT!
MEDIEVAL FASHION

The Irish and the Normans dressed and wore their hair very differently from each other. You would be able to identify who was who from a good distance away – a bit like how you can recognise someone from another school by the colour of their uniform.

The Irish at the time were very fond of saffron – a dye made from a plant that gave clothing a golden yellow colour. It's thought that Irish people wore saffron as much as modern people wear blue jeans – that's how common it was. The Normans dressed in the latest fashions and some of these were pretty wacky as we'll see later. Their clothes were brightly dyed all sorts of colours, usually because they wanted to show off how wealthy they were as certain dyes could be very expensive and were usually imported from other countries.

If modern plastic dolls and action figures were around back then, we might have seen some like these ...

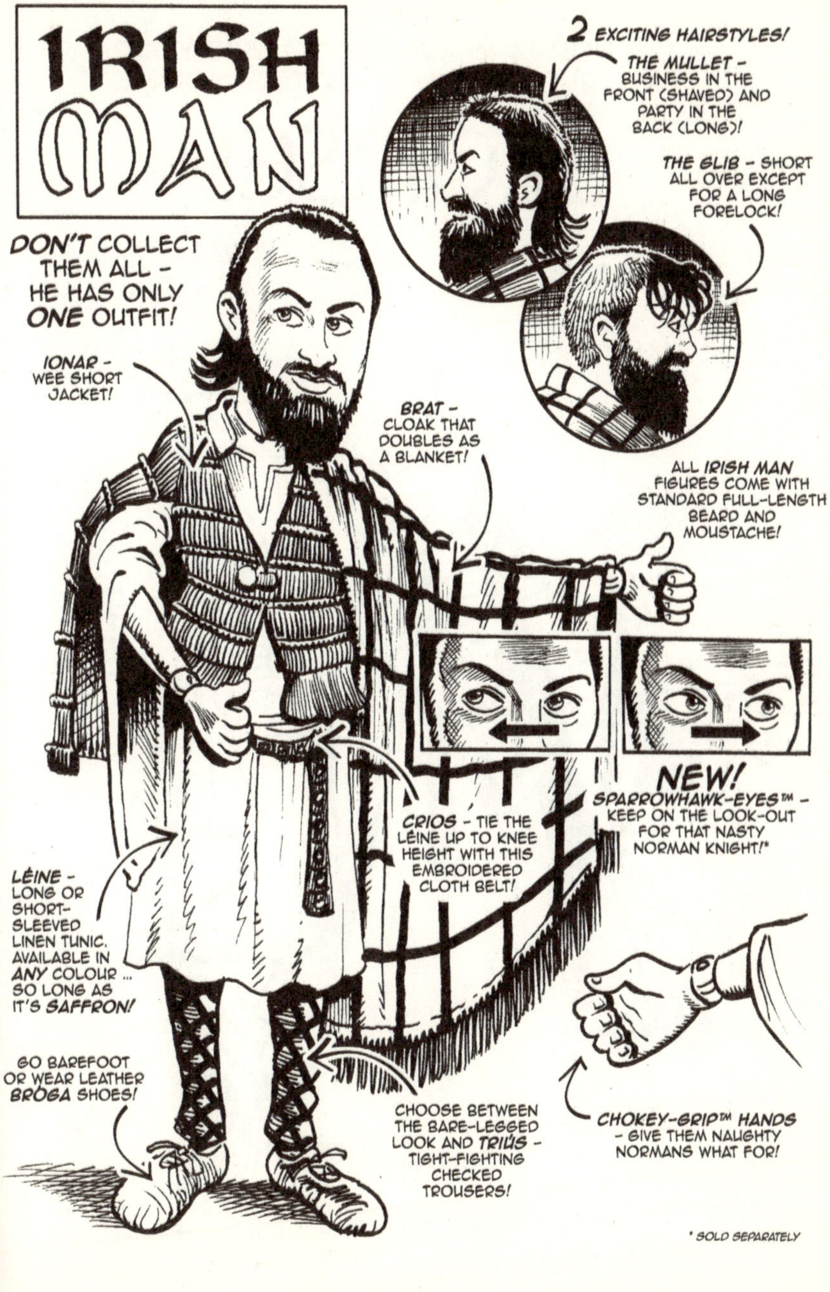
IRISH MAN
DON'T COLLECT THEM ALL - HE HAS ONLY ONE OUTFIT!
2 EXCITING HAIRSTYLES!
THE MULLET - BUSINESS IN THE FRONT (SHAVED) AND PARTY IN THE BACK (LONG)!
THE GLIB - SHORT ALL OVER EXCEPT FOR A LONG FORELOCK!
IONAR - WEE SHORT JACKET!
BRAT - CLOAK THAT DOUBLES AS A BLANKET!
ALL IRISH MAN FIGURES COME WITH STANDARD FULL-LENGTH BEARD AND MOUSTACHE!
NEW! SPARROWHAWK-EYES™ - KEEP ON THE LOOK-OUT FOR THAT NASTY NORMAN KNIGHT!*
CRIOS - TIE THE LÉINE UP TO KNEE HEIGHT WITH THIS EMBROIDERED CLOTH BELT!
LÉINE - LONG OR SHORT-SLEEVED LINEN TUNIC. AVAILABLE IN ANY COLOUR ... SO LONG AS IT'S SAFFRON!
GO BAREFOOT OR WEAR LEATHER BRÓGA SHOES!
CHOOSE BETWEEN THE BARE-LEGGED LOOK AND TRIÚS - TIGHT-FIGHTING CHECKED TROUSERS!
CHOKEY-GRIP™ HANDS - GIVE THEM NAUGHTY NORMANS WHAT FOR!
* SOLD SEPARATELY

THE NORMANS MAY TRY TO TAKE YOUR LIFE, BUT THEY'LL NEVER TAKE YOUR ...

SAOIRSE!

CAULDRON, LOOM AND COW SOLD SEPARATELY.

I AM ... NORMAN KNIGHT

I'VE GOT **2** EXCITING OUTFITS! BATTLE ARMOUR AND EVENING WEAR ... OR SHOULD I SAY *KNIGHT* WEAR! *HA!*

AFTER A HARD DAY OF GIVING THOSE IRISH A GOOD HIDING, I LIKE TO RELAX IN *BRIGHTLY COLOURED, FINELY TAILORED* CLOTHING!
ANYTHING BUT *SAFFRON!* HA HA HA!

I HAVE **2** COOL HAIRSTYLES TO CHOOSE FROM - THE PUDDING BOWL AND THE SHAVED-AT-THE-BACK LOOK AS SEEN ON THE BAYEUX TAPESTRY!

POINTY HELMET!
SWORD!
CHAIN-MAIL HAUBERK!
TUNIC!
BELT!
SHIELD!
HOSE!
BOOTS!

SET INCLUDES STICKERS TO MAKE YOUR OWN SHIELD DESIGN. WINE GOBLET AND GOSHAWK SOLD SEPARATELY.

NO CASTLE IS COMPLETE WITHOUT AN ELEGANT LADY AND THERE'S NO LADY LIKE ...

LADY ELEANOR

5 THRILLING LOOKS!

1) HAIR IN PLAITS BOUND WITH RIBBONS, THE ENDS ENCASED IN SILVER CYLINDERS!

2) TWO-HORNED SILK HENIN HEADDRESS!

3) JEWELLED CIRCLET!

4) BROAD-BRIMMED FELT HAT WITH WIMPLE & VEIL FOR GOING OUT IN THE ALL-TOO-RARE IRISH SUNSHINE!

5) STEEPLED HENIN WITH LOOSE VEIL!

LADY ELEANOR'S FINE SILK GOWN FLOWS ELEGANTLY TO THE FLOOR AND IS GATHERED AT THE WAIST BY A STUNNING EMBROIDERED GIRDLE. LONG, STREAMING SLEEVES EDGED WITH JEWELLED EMBROIDERY ENSURE *LADY ELEANOR* MAKES ALL THE RIGHT SWISHING SOUNDS AS SHE SASHAYS AROUND THE BANQUET HALL. HER PORCELAIN SKIN IS KEPT WARM AGAINST THE HARSH IRISH CLIMATE BY A LUXURIOUS MANTLE, MADE OF THE FINEST WOOL. ONCE YOU'VE PLAYED WITH THIS BEAUTIFUL LIMITED EDITION* *LADY ELEANOR* DOLL, NOTHING ELSE WILL EVER DO!

* ONLY FIVE MILLION PRODUCED. HURRY AND ORDER YOURS TODAY!

Just like nowadays, fashion was constantly changing. You might be surprised to learn that in late medieval Ireland, some people wore a hoodie! This was called a *cochall*. They also wore a hooded cloak called a *fallaing*. Some hoodies had a long point on the end called a *liripipe* that had to be draped over one shoulder.

fallaing

cochall

liripipe

The Normans wore shoes with pointy toes called *poulaines*. Over time, they got more and more pointed. The longer they were, the more important the wearer was. Sometimes they were so long, the points had to be tied to the shins with a little chain. There's a story about French knights at the Battle of Nicopolis in 1396 who had to cut off the points of their shoes before they could run away from their attackers! Here's a selection of medieval shoes ...

Poulaines – nobility are permitted two-foot lengths, merchants one-foot length and peasants, half.

For wet and muddy streets, wooden soles, or pattens, can be tied to your shoes.

From the 1470s to the early 1500s, men's shoes became wider with rounded, puffed toes.

Women's shoes did not change much over the years as they were always hidden under long dresses.

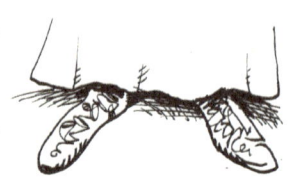

Irish people went barefoot or wore leather *bróga*.

ODD JOBS
WORK AND TRADE

There were loads of jobs that people did both inside castles and towns and also in the countryside, which is where the majority of the native Irish lived. Many of the jobs seem a bit strange to us because we have machines and factories that do a lot of the difficult, dangerous work. Most jobs back then had to be done by hand. People made their own clothes, grew their own food and worked long hours.

Older children could become an apprentice and learn a trade. It took a long time – usually seven years – before their apprenticeship was complete. Apprentices lived with their masters who taught them all they needed to know. They weren't usually paid, but they did receive free food, clothes and a roof over their heads. The apprentice qualified when they produced a 'masterpiece' that showed off his or her skills. After their apprenticeship, they were free to set up their own business.

Some businesses you might recognise like blacksmiths, tailors, carpenters and bakers but others you may not be so familiar with. Can you match the trade to its description? **Answers below.**

A) Cooper
B) Miller
C) Farrier
D) Weaver
E) Apothecary
F) Chandler

1. A type of blacksmith who made horseshoes and nails and shoed horses.
2. A person who dispensed herbs and medicines.
3. Someone who made candles.
4. A craftsman who made barrels.
5. Someone who made cloth.
6. A person who ground grain to make flour.

ANSWERS: A) 4. B) 6. C) 1. D) 5. E) 2. F) 3.

Some street names in cities like Dublin reflect what trade was carried on there. Cook Street was where bakers sold their breads and pies. It was located just outside the city walls so that sparks from their ovens wouldn't start fires. You could buy fish from a fishmonger fresh out of the Liffey on Fishamble Street. Because few people could read, street signs hung outside shops so people knew what they sold. Can you guess what these shops were from their signs? **Answers below.**

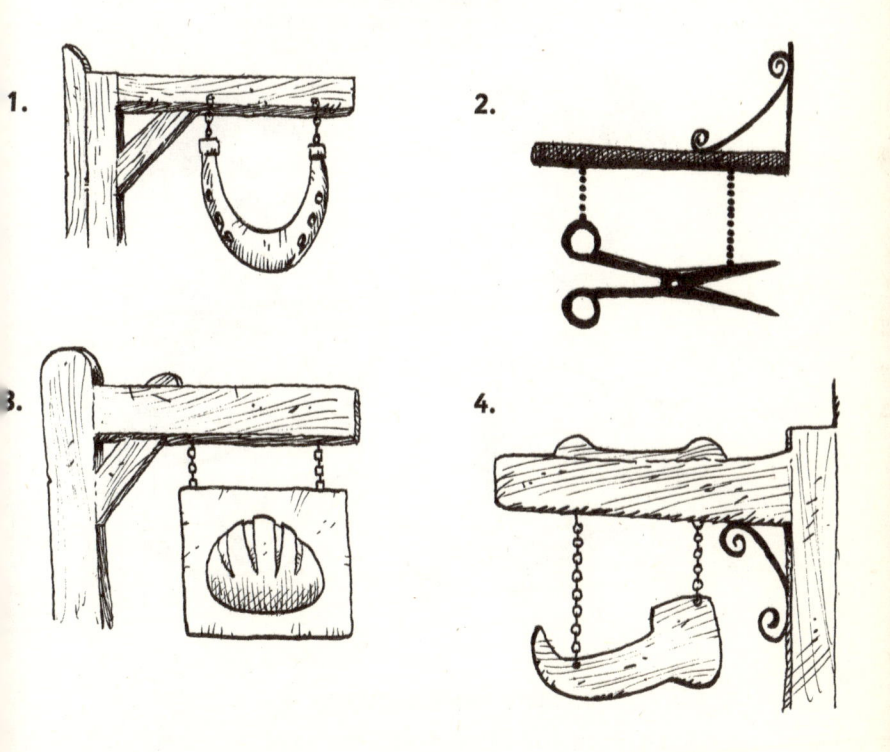

1.

2.

3.

4.

ANSWERS: 1) Farrier. 2) Tailor. 3) Baker. 4) Shoemaker.

In the 13th century, Dublin held a great fair at Fair Green where merchants from other parts of the world set up their stalls to do business. Rich people could buy fine silks and spices from Asia and sugar from Africa. People called scribes, who could read and write, sold their services to draw up legal documents. Scribes called *pardoners* even sold forgiveness for sins you might commit in the future!

Of course, there were plenty of less popular jobs available both for adults and for eager children just starting out on a professional career ...

APPRENTICE FULLER WANTED

Strong child needed to tread cloth in a vat of stale urine and clay for up to ten hours a day. Disgusting, smelly, boring work but don't let your mind wander! All parts of the cloth have to be trod on equally to make the cloth softer and the gaps between fibres smaller.

DEADLY! DATA: Human urine contains ammonia, a chemical that stinks to high heaven but has great cleaning properties

SPIT-BOY NEEDED

(Nothing to do with spitting, so don't get excited.)

You will be a member of a team of hard-working scullions in a busy castle kitchen, turning roasting meat on a spit for hours on end to ensure it's cooked. Your hands will certainly blister but a bale of stinky wet hay is provided to shield against the roaring flames. You're welcome.

DEADLY! DATA: The spit-boy is the lowliest job in the castle kitchen and it's hot, sweaty, boring work. In later years, turnspit dogs were used to power treadmills that turned the meat.

POSITION VACANT – LEECH COLLECTOR

Willing man or woman required to walk bare-legged in marshland so medicinal leeches* can attach themselves to feet and legs. One or two are no good – we need **HUNDREDS!**

DEADLY! DATA: Leeches leave welts and because your legs bleed constantly you will feel dizzy or even pass out. The wounds can become infected. Leech collecting can only be done in warmer weather so at least you'll get a tan. (As long as it doesn't rain, which it will, because it's Ireland.)

BRAIGTEOIR REQUIRED

Professional flatulist (farter) needed for long evenings of entertainment at his lordship's tower house. Applicants must be able to fart a wide range of tunes. (Free cabbage, beans and pickled onions provided before every performance.)

DEADLY! DATA: Though *braigteoir* were not as highly regarded in medieval Irish society as other entertainers such as harpists and storytellers, they were still very well paid. They are mentioned in the 12th-century Tech Midchúarda – a diagram of the royal feasting hall at Tara.

---

* See what medicinal leeches were used for on page 92. They're now extinct in Ireland.

TANNER APPRENTICES URGENTLY NEEDED

Want to work in a job that's the dirtiest, smelliest, grossest trade of all? Then look no further! We will teach you all you need to know about **tanning** – preparing animal skins to make leather. You will learn how to ...

FETCH stinking animal hides from the slaughterhouse!

SOAK the hides in stale pee!

SCUDD (scrape off) blood, flesh and fur!

BATE (soften) the hides by pounding them in dog and bird poo!

DEADLY! DATA: The job of tanning stank so much that tanners often had to work on the outskirts of town. They could never get rid of the awful stench from their clothes, skin and hair and often ended up having to marry others in the same trade.

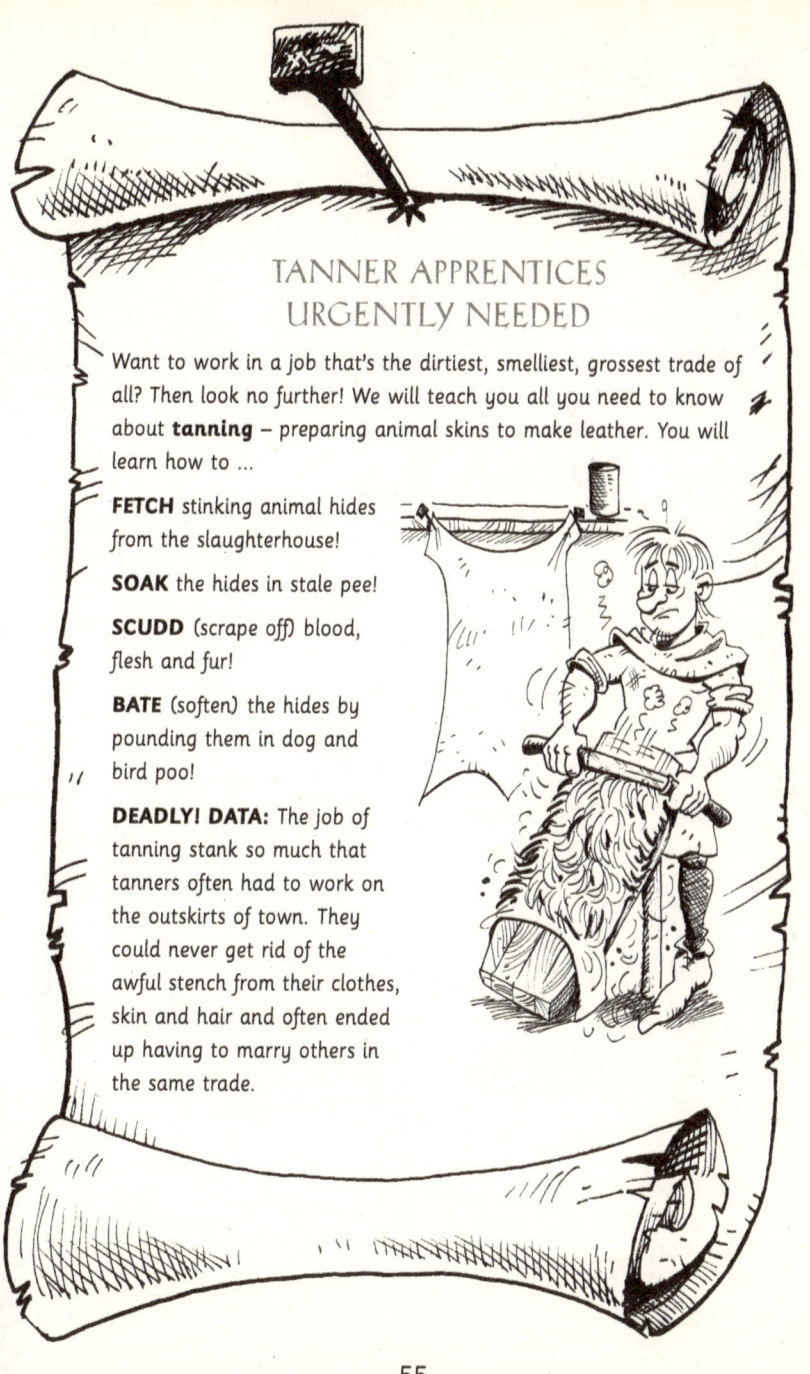

FAMOUS IRISH CASTLES #2*

BLARNEY CASTLE CO. CORK
6

CENTURY BUILT: 12TH
HAUNTED: 0
DEADLINESS: 7

Home of the famous Blarney Stone (said to grant anyone who kisses it the 'gift of the gab'), the castle has a curse upon it. Anyone who removes a stone, rock or even a pebble from the area will have misery and misfortune for the rest of their lives.

CAHIR CASTLE CO. TIPPERARY
8

CENTURY BUILT: 13TH
HAUNTED: 👻
DEADLINESS: 9

This is one of Ireland's biggest and b[est] preserved castles and has been feat[ured in] loads of films and TV shows. It is bu[ilt on a] rocky island in the river Suir. There[is a] cannonball lodged in one of the ca[stle's] towers that's been there since a sie[ge in] 1599.

ENNISCORTHY CASTLE CO. WEXFORD
20

CENTURY BUILT: 12TH
HAUNTED: 👻
DEADLINESS: 6

This castle was built by the Norman knight Philip de Prendergast and was attacked by the Leinster king Art MacMurrough in order to get his family's lands back. It was used as a prison in the 1798 Rebellion. A local ghost-hunting group made contact with a spirit named Jim who was alive in the early 1900s.

ATHLONE CASTLE CO. WESTMEATH
1

CENTURY BUILT: 12TH
HAUNTED: 0
DEADLINESS: 7

Now home to the Athlone Visitor Centre, the Normans built this castle at an important crossing point on the River Shannon. The central tower of the castle collapsed a year after it was built, killing nine men. The Great Siege of Athlone took place here in 1691, and 12,000 cannonballs were fired over ten days – that's about one every two minutes!

CARRICKFERGUS CASTLE CO. ANTRIM

10

CENTURY BUILT: 12TH
HAUNTED: 🌼🌼
DEADLINESS: 7

Built by the Norman knight John de Courcy, this impressive castle played an important military role until 1928. It is haunted by Buttoncap, a soldier who was wrongly executed for murder. Just before he was executed he swore to haunt the castle forever.

JOHNSTOWN CASTLE CO. WEXFORD

26

CENTURY BUILT: 12TH
HAUNTED: 0
DEADLINESS: 7

Built by the Esmondes, a noble Norman family, this stunning castle is now home to the Irish Agricultural Museum and 150 acres of beautiful gardens. The 86-metre servants' tunnel that runs under the castle is the longest in Ireland. Servants' tunnels were used by castle staff so that the nobles they served weren't disturbed by them. Nobody wants to see a scruffy servant now, do they?

WHITE'S CASTLE CO. KILDARE

40

CENTURY BUILT: 15TH
HAUNTED: 🌼
DEADLINESS: 5

This tower house was built to protect the new bridge over the river Barrow. It served as the local jail in the 18th century and was notorious for its terrible conditions. A ghostly figure has been seen peering out of a window on the second floor.

KING JOHN'S CASTLE CO. LIMERICK

30

CENTURY BUILT: 13TH
HAUNTED: 0
DEADLINESS: 7

Built on the site of an old Viking stronghold on the river Shannon, this castle has a huge gatehouse and circular corner towers. The castle is named for King John, Henry II's son who was made Lord of Ireland when he was just nine. He is the king who Robin Hood fights against in all the stories.

* See map, page 138.

THIS ONE WILL SLAY YOU

WAR AND FIGHTING

There was really nothing more fearsome than a Norman knight. He had the best weapons and armour available at the time. When the Normans landed at Wexford they easily took down Irish warriors who, we're told, could only hurl rocks at them.

Noble boys aged around seven were sent to a lord's household to start their combat training as pages. When they were about fourteen, they could become a squire. At age twenty-one, they could become a knight.

Thanks to the Bayeux Tapestry (see page 14), we know what a lot of these weapons looked like. I could show you the weapons a Norman knight used but we'll let a 'used-weapons salesman' do all the talking ...

Ye Olde Used Weapons Shoppe
V.V. d'Odgy (prop.)
purveyor of quality weapons since 1172
SEE ANYTHING YOU LIKE, SIR?
JUST HAVING A LOOK, REALLY. I WAS KNIGHTED LAST WEEK AND ...
... AND A FINE KNIGHT LIKE YOU WANTS THE FINEST WEAPONS! SAY NO MORE, SIR! RIGHT THIS WAY!
SWISH!
ER, WELL ...
YOU'LL BE NEEDING A NICE, LONG LANCE, SIR! PERFECT FOR IMPALING IRISHMEN FROM HORSEBACK! GREAT VALUE FOR MONEY TOO!
UM ...
UH, OK – I'LL TAKE IT!
DEADLY! DATA:
SHAFT MADE FROM ASH WOOD.
275–425 CM LONG.
LEAF-SHAPED IRON OR STEEL HEAD.
PENNANT WITH KNIGHT'S SYMBOL OR COAT OF ARMS*.

*SEE PAGE 62

NOT THIS ONE, SIR! THIS IS FOR DISPLAY ONLY. ARTHUR, GET THE GOOD KNIGHT A NICE LANCE FROM OUT THE BACK!
WINK!
More weapons this way
CERTAINLY, V.V.!
WINK!
STAFF
A BRAVE KNIGHT LIKE YOU CAN'T BE SEEN WITHOUT A SWORD! THEY'RE A TAD PRICEY ...
DEADLY! DATA: MADE FROM IRON OR STEEL. AROUND 76 CM LONG. BROAD, DOUBLE-EDGED BLADE. CROSS-GUARD PROTECTS THE HAND.
... BUT ONCE YOU SLICE OFF AN IRISHMAN'S HEAD YOU'LL KNOW WHERE THAT EXTRA MONEY WENT, SIR!
I CAN'T REALLY AFFORD ...
EXACTLY, SIR – YOU CAN'T AFFORD NOT TO HAVE A SWORD!
AND YOU CAN'T HAVE A SWORD WITHOUT A SHIELD!
DEADLY! DATA: MADE FROM WOOD AND COVERED WITH LEATHER. 115CM LONG AND KITE-SHAPED TO PROTECT THE WHOLE BODY. METAL BOSS TO PROTECT THE HAND. PAINTED WITH KNIGHT'S SYMBOL OR COAT OF ARMS.
WELL, I SUPPOSE ...

I HEAR THOSE IRISH ARE PRETTY GOOD AT THROWING STONES! YOU DON'T WANT TO TAKE A STONE TO THE OLD *NOGGIN*, DO YOU, SIR?

DEADLY! DATA: POINTED HELMET MADE FROM IRON OR STEEL. GUARD TO PROTECT THE NOSE.

HERE'S THE *BAD BOY* OF THE WEAPON WORLD, SIR – THE *CROSSBOW!* THE CHURCH TRIED TO *BAN* THIS, Y'KNOW!*

DEADLY! DATA: MADE FROM YEW WOOD. 75 CM LONG. FIRES ARROWS CALLED BOLTS OR QUARRELS.

THAT LAD IS AS *GREEN* AS A BAG OF CABBAGES. I EVEN SOLD HIM A 'HORSE'!

YOU CAN'T PUT A KNIGHT OUT ON A DOG LIKE THAT!**

CHING CHING!

SCAFF

*BUT ONLY WHEN USED AGAINST CHRISTIANS. ANYONE ELSE WAS FAIR GAME!

** PUNCHLINE COURTESY OF *YE OLDE JOKE BOOKE.*

Knights had their own **coats of arms** (symbols and colours that they wore over their armour and on their shields) so they could be identified on the battlefield – a bit like how a football team has its badge. The difference between a knight and a football team is that a football team is not bleeding to death at the end of the game ... well, not usually.

A coat of arms tends to be shield-shaped with a motto (a short sentence that describes the knight's values) below. Some shields are divided in two, three or four, with a different symbol in each section.

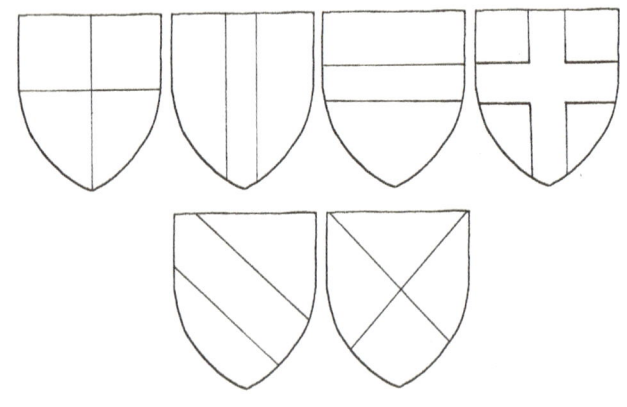

Copy the shield shape on the next page to make your own coat of arms. In the olden days, a family symbol might be a powerful animal like a lion, but you draw whatever you think sums you up: a football, a superhero or your pet goldfish. Then add a motto to go in the banner below the shield. Maybe it's a phrase you use a lot, or your favourite song lyrics – anything at all!

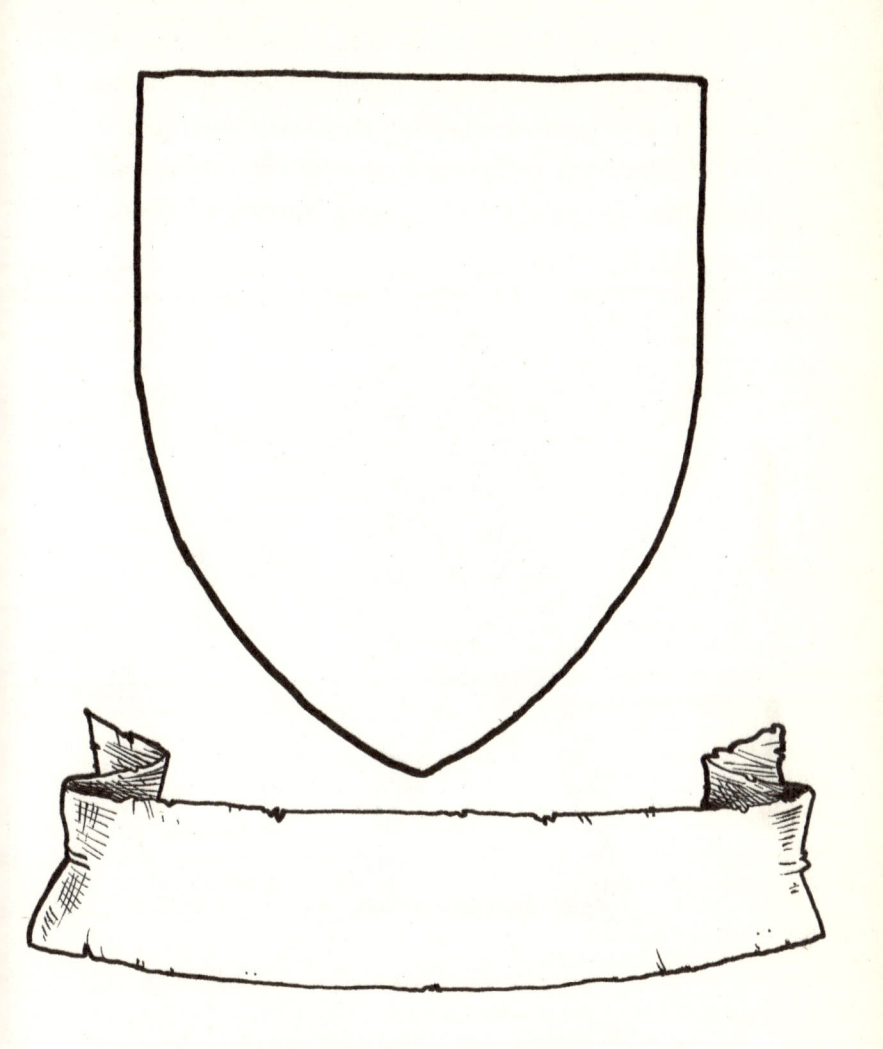

You could spend some time researching your real family coat of arms – most families have one!

This is Alice of Abergavenny, also known as Alice the Vicious. She was among the Normans who fought the Irish in the Battle of Baginbun Head near Waterford in 1170. She didn't get her nickname for her charity work but does she tell big, fat whoppers? **Answers below.**

A) I CUT OFF THE HEADS OF THIRTY IRISH PRISONERS BECAUSE MY BOYFRIEND WAS KILLED BY THE IRISH IN THE BATTLE.

C) ALTHOUGH THE IRISH HAD BETWEEN 3,000 AND 4,000 MEN, JUST 200 NORMANS DEFEATED THEM.

B) WE DEFEATED THE IRISH WITH THE HELP OF THEIR OWN COWS.

D) MY REAL JOB WAS AS A SERVANT GIRL.

E) WE THREW ALL THE HEADLESS IRISH SOLDIERS INTO A LAKE.

ANSWERS: Alice may be vicious, but she only lied a couple of times. a) False. She actually beheaded *seventy* men with an axe – in one afternoon! b) Yep. A poem from the 13th century called *The Song of Dermot and the Earl* tells us that the Norman leader, Raymond le Gros, unleashed a herd of stolen Irish cows to break through the Irish army's ranks. c) False. The Normans were the best fighters of their day. It took just 100 of them to beat the Irish. d) Yup! Alice's day job was waitressing. e) Nope! They threw them off a cliff.

DEADLY! CRAFTY SWORD

1) Draw two 45 cm-long parallel lines, 3 cm apart, on cardboard.

2) At one end of the lines, measure 1.5 cm towards the middle and put a dot 5 cm from there out past the end of the lines. Draw a triangle from the end of the lines to the dot to make the pointy end of the sword.

3) Draw around a mug at the other end of the lines to make a semicircle for the hilt (handle) and pommel (the round bit at the end of a sword).

4) Repeat with another piece of card, cut out both shapes and glue together.

5) Take a piece of tin foil the same length as your blade and glue it to one side, wrapping it tightly around the blade, taking care not to tear it, and stick down the end.

6) Draw an oval on a piece of thick card (10 X 6 cm). Cut a slot out of the middle of it that's the same size as your blade. This is the cross guard part of your sword that protects the hand.

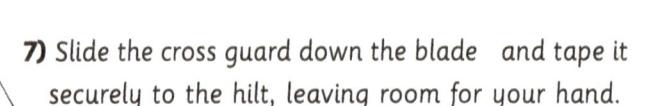

7) Slide the cross guard down the blade and tape it securely to the hilt, leaving room for your hand.

8) Wind silver or black tape around the hilt all the way up to the pommel.

9) Draw a line with a black marker down the centre of the blade. This is called the 'fuller' or 'blood gutter' because blood would drain down it. Coooool!

10) Give your sword a DEADLY! name like 'Widowmaker' or 'Dragon Fang'.

Don't go charging off into battle just yet because you need one more thing ...

DEADLY! CRAFTY SHIELD

1) Take a sheet of cardboard and draw a shield shape. (The Normans had big, long kite-shaped shields, but you can make your shield whatever shape and size you want.)

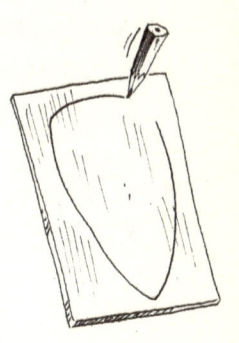

2) Cut out the shield shape.

3) Draw around this shape onto another sheet of thick card and cut it out. You now have two shield shapes the same size.

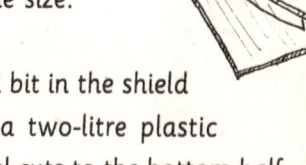

4) To make the boss (the round bit in the shield that protects the hand), cut a two-litre plastic bottle in half and make six equal cuts to the bottom half.

5) Draw a circle around the bottom of the bottle about a third of the way down on one of the pieces of cardboard.

6) Cut out the circle. Push the bottle through the hole and bend over the cut plastic bits then tape or glue them to the cardboard. Then glue the other cardboard piece on top of that.

7) Paint the shield in the Norman style. They usually had their coat of arms painted on theirs (see page 62). Paint the boss and shield edge silver.

8) Cut two strips of thick card for a handle (about 8 x 30 cm each). Fold them as shown and tape them to the back around the same height as the boss on the other side.

Now you can charge into battle!

DEADLY! CRAFTY CROSSBOW

Some soldiers used crossbows in battle. These were very **DEADLY!** weapons and extremely accurate. Here's how to make your own slightly less lethal version.

1) Take two unsharpened pencils the same length and tightly wrap a rubber band around them about 2 cm from each end. This is called the stock.

2) Repeat with another two pencils. This is called the lathe.

3) Place the lathe on top of the stock, forming a cross shape, and secure tightly with two more rubber bands. Make sure it forms a perfect cross and isn't wonky or else it won't fire straight.

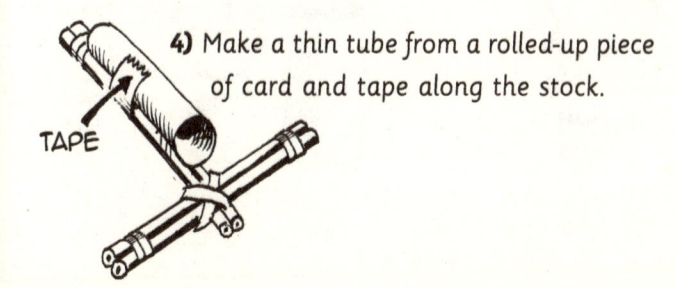

4) Make a thin tube from a rolled-up piece of card and tape along the stock.

TAPE

5) Loop a large rubber band around each end of one of the pencils in the lathe. These are the bowstrings.

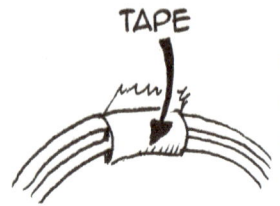

TAPE

6) Take a piece of tape and stick it around the centre of the bowstrings.

7) Use drinking straws as bolts (crossbow arrows). Insert into the tube, pull back the bowstrings and voilà – you got yourself a crossbow! Use toilet roll tubes as targets.

IRISH WEAPONS AND ARMOUR

A stone.

Only kidding. The Irish also used:

Axes   Swords

Helmets

Small shields
(called bucklers)

Spears

But against a fully armoured Norman knight on horseback, they might as well have just been throwing stones.

FAMOUS IRISH CASTLES #3*

DUNGUAIRE CASTLE CO. GALWAY

18

CENTURY BUILT: 16TH
HAUNTED: 0
DEADLINESS: 5

This castle was built by the O'Hynes clan on the site of the fortress of the legendary Connacht King Guaire. The king was said to be so generous that his skeletal hand reached out of his grave and dropped gold coins at the feet of a beggar. According to folklore, if a person stands at the front gate of the castle and asks a question, they will have an answer by the end of the day.

KILCOE CASTLE CO. CORK

28

CENTURY BUILT: 15TH
HAUNTED: 0
DEADLINESS: 5

The McCarthy clan built this castle on an island in Roaringwater Bay. It was built in such a strategic location that it took English troops a long time to capture it in the early 1600s. Jeremy Irons, a famous English actor, restored the castle and had it painted in orangey hues which not everyone liked.

THOOR BALLYLEE CASTLE CO. GALWAY

37

CENTURY BUILT: 15TH
HAUNTED: 👻👻
DEADLINESS: 6

The famous Irish poet, author and playwright W.B. Yeats and his family once lived in this fortified tower house, also known as Yeats's Tower. He called a book of his poems *The Tower* after it and believed his home was haunted by the ghost of a Norman soldier. A famous photo taken in 1989 shows the figure of a ghostly boy. The photographer insisted there was no one there when he took the picture.

MALAHIDE CASTLE CO. DUBLIN

32

CENTURY BUILT: 12TH
HAUNTED: 👻👻👻👻
DEADLINESS: 9

This beautiful castle was owned by the same family – the Talbots – for 800 years. It also has four botanical gardens with thousands of plants from all over the world. The castle is said to have at least five ghosts, one of whom was a jester called Puck who was stabbed to death. With his dying breath, he vowed to haunt the castle.

CLONONY CASTLE CO. OFFALY

14

CENTURY BUILT: 15TH
HAUNTED: ☘☘☘
DEADLINESS: 6

Henry VIII gave this castle to Thomas Boleyn for his daughter Anne's hand in marriage. Henry later married Anne and then had her head cut off. The graves of two of Anne's nieces were found here. The castle is haunted by the Thin Man who appears on the roof surrounded by a strange fog.

DONEGAL CASTLE CO. DONEGAL

16

CENTURY BUILT: 15TH
HAUNTED: 0
DEADLINESS: 6

Red Hugh O'Donnell of the powerful O'Donnell clan – rulers of the Tír Chonaill kingdom for over 400 years – built this castle as a fortress. Red Hugh vowed never to let the castle fall into English hands, so he burned it down. But English captain Sir Basil Brooke became the castle's new lord in 1616.

BUNRATTY CASTLE CO. CLARE

7

CENTURY BUILT: 13TH
HAUNTED: ☘
DEADLINESS: 8

This is the fourth castle to be built on or near the site, originally a Viking trading post. In the 15th century, it became the stronghold of the O'Briens, the largest clan in North Munster. A 17th-century visitor to the castle was woken in the night by a red-haired banshee floating outside her bedroom window – which was several storeys up! You can dine at a medieval banquet in the castle.

FERNS CASTLE CO. WEXFORD

22

CENTURY BUILT: 13TH
HAUNTED: 0
DEADLINESS: 5

Built by the famous Norman knight, William Marshal, this square-shaped castle once had four round towers, one at each corner. One of the remaining towers contains a beautiful circular chapel. In the visitors' centre you can see a 15-metre-long tapestry, sewn by locals to illustrate the history of Ferns. The castle was built on the site of Diarmuid MacMurrough's fortress. He was the Irish king who invited the Normans to Ireland.

* See map, page 138.

MEDIEVAL AND MEDIGOOD
CRIME AND PUNISHMENT

The Normans only ever conquered around two-thirds of Ireland and over time they started losing power. In the 14th century, the English king Edward III sent his son Lionel to investigate. By then the Normans had been in Ireland for about two hundred years and were known as Anglo-Irish. Young Lionel was horrified. He could hardly tell the Anglo-Irish and the Irish apart. They spoke Irish, dressed like the Irish and lived under the Irish Brehon laws*. To whip the settlers into shape, Lionel made a set of harsh laws called *The Statutes of Kilkenny*. It was forbidden to:

- Marry an Irish person
- Adopt an Irish child
- Use an Irish name
- Wear Irish clothes
- Speak the Irish language
- Play Irish music
- Listen to Irish storytellers
- Play Irish games
- Ride a horse in Irish style (without a saddle)

To break any of the laws was to be guilty of treason and could be punished by death. Guess what? Nobody paid a blind bit of notice!

* See *Deadly! Irish History – The Celts*.

The settlers still loyal to the English Crown had retreated to just four counties in the east – Dublin, Meath, Louth and Kildare – and these 'obedient shires' were the only parts of Ireland still under English control. These were fenced off from the rest of Ireland with wooden stakes called pales and the area became known as the Pale. As time went on, they built a deep ditch surrounded by high earthen banks on each side and ringed by thorny hedges to protect against Irish attacks and raids.

The people who lived within the Pale were protected by the English Crown, but if they went outside it they lost that protection. They were 'beyond the pale', which has become a modern expression to mean 'unacceptable behaviour'.

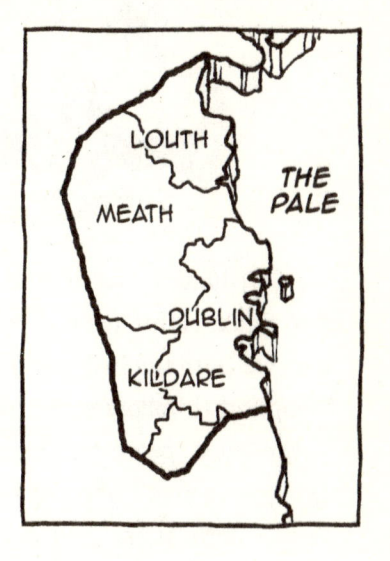

Before Saint Patrick brought Christianity to Ireland in the fifth century, the native Irish believed that when they died, they went to a place called the Otherworld, stayed there awhile, then returned to Earth in a new body. This was called reincarnation. Death wasn't something they feared.

Christianity taught that you had only one life and that you'd better live well or else you might not get into heaven. Both the Irish and the Normans were Christians. They had to follow strict rules set down by the Church – the most powerful force in medieval Ireland. The Normans weren't allowed to invade Ireland without the Pope's permission, and many bishops in Ireland were rich beyond belief.

While the native Irish lived under the ancient Brehon laws, the Normans had their own legal system. Noble officials called *justicars* appointed *seneshals* (or stewards) to dispense justice. They usually favoured other nobles over poorer people and the Norman settlers over the native Irish. There was a lot of injustice in medieval Ireland.

They had some imaginative punishments for people who broke the law in medieval Ireland. Let's play a little game to find out what they were ...

IT'S LANDED IN THE PILLORY! LET'S HAVE A LOOK AT THAT!
CLACK CLACKKITY CLACK!
THE PILLORY
WHAT DO YA THINK, DÁITHÍ? DO YA FANCY THE PILLORY WHERE PEOPLE GET TO SHOUT ABUSE AND PELT YOU WITH ROTTEN EGGS ALL DAY?
WHIFF!
PONG!
LIKE THE ONE AT THE CROSSROADS NEAR CHRIST CHURCH CATHEDRAL IN DUBLIN?
BOB - MAIRTÍN'S GLAMOROUS ASSISTANT!
NO - ME MA WOULD KILL ME, MAIRTÍN! I'LL PLAY ON.
HE'S PLAYIN' ON! GIVE HIM A ROUND OF APPLAUSE, FOLKS!
CLAP CLAP CLAP!
A FINE! THE MOST COMMON PUNISHMENT IN MEDIEVAL IRELAND! WHAT DO YOU THINK, DÁITHÍ? DO YA WANT TO PAY A FINE OR DO YA WANT TO PLAY ON?
CLACKKITY CLACK-CLACK!
A FINE
I WOULD PAY A FINE, MAIRTÍN, BUT I'M COMPLETELY SKINT!
I'LL HAVE TO PLAY ON.
EMPTY!
...NADA!

BY JAPERS, IT'S THE STOCKS!
STOCKS
CLACK CLACKKITY CLACK!
AT LEAST YOU'D GET TO SIT DOWN, DÁITHÍ BUT YOU COULD BE THERE FOR DAYS! AND YOU'RE NOT ALLOWED A CUSHION!
MA
WHAT DO YA THINK, FOLKS? SHOULD HE TAKE THE STOCKS OR PLAY ON?
DON'T BE AN EEJIT DÁITHÍ!
DO THE TIME, DON'T PAY THE FINE!
SURE IT'S ONLY THE ONE EYE DÁITHÍ!
PLAY ON!
PLAY ON!
PLAY ON!
PLAY ON!
I'LL CHANCE IT, MAIRTÍN. PLAY ON!
HE'S CRUMBLED UNDER AUDIENCE PRESSURE! TWO SPINS LEFT!
A FINE
YAAAAYYYY!!!
OOOOH! IT'S BLINDING IN ONE EYE, DÁITHÍ! A PUNISHMENT SOME IRISH KINGS GAVE OUT TO NE'ER-DO-WELLS LIKE YOURSELF!*
BLINDING IN ONE EYE
*DIARMUID MACMURROUGH WAS WELL KNOWN FOR DOING THIS.

WHAT DO YA THINK, DÁITHÍ? WOULD YA LIKE TO BE BLINDED IN THE ONE EYE?
THE STOCKS
SIZZLE!
FREEDOM
NO - I DON'T THINK I'D FANCY THAT. I'LL PLAY ON.
HUFF!
THE STOCKS
FREEDOM
MA
EXCITING STUFF INDEED! ONE FINAL SPIN, NOW, DÁITHÍ! WHAT'LL IT BE?
CLAKKITY CLACK CLACK ... CLACK...
YESSS!! GET IN!
WHAT ABOUT THAT!?! IT'S LANDED IN FREEDOM! WELL DONE, DAI-
OH JANEY MAC! THE BALL'S HOPPED OUT!
THE GALLOWS
GULP!
BAD LUCK, DÁITHÍ! HANGING WAS A COMMON PUNISHMENT FOR CRIMINALS FOUND GUILTY OF SEVERE CRIMES. WHAT DID YOU DO ANYWAY?
DROPPED LITTER!
MA

Meet Henry Tyrel, an outlaw who caused mayhem in counties Dublin and Kildare in the 14th century – a bit like an Irish Robin Hood. He may be outside the law, but does this make Henry a liar too? **Answers below.**

A) JUST LIKE ROBIN HOOD, I ROB FROM THE RICH TO GIVE TO THE POOR.

C) AFTER I COMMIT CRIMES IN CO. DUBLIN, I FLEE OVER THE BORDER TO CO. KILDARE BECAUSE THE SENESHAL THERE CAN'T ARREST ME FOR CRIMES I COMMIT IN DUBLIN.

B) I COME FROM A POOR FAMILY.

D) I WILL PROBABLY BE HANGED FOR MY CRIMES.

ANSWERS: Henry is a bit of a rogue. He lied every time but one. a) Afraid not. Henry robbed from everyone and kept it for himself. b) Nope – his father Gerald was a wealthy knight. So why did he feel the need to steal? Because he was not the eldest son and so didn't inherit his father's wealth. To live the life he wanted, he stole from others. c) True. When he committed crimes in Kildare, he fled over the border to Dublin for the same reason. He eventually got caught, though. d) Henry is a little optimistic. He was actually sentenced to death by starvation in Dublin Castle jail.

YOU WANT ME TO EAT WHAT?!?
FOOD AND DRINK

In late medieval times the foods that the rich and the poor ate were very different. A book of accounts from 1338 lists the ingredients for dinner and supper that Gilbert de Bolyniop, Prior of Christ Church Cathedral in Dublin, had one evening: baked meat pasties, roast lamb, chicken and beef, along with expensive breads made from fine flour, all washed down with lots of good wine. These ingredients cost more than half a poor man's annual wages.

The Normans had exotic tastes. Sometimes their menu had not only meat fritters (a pie made from animal entrails), salted eels, pigeon, swan, heron, kid (young goat), gosling (young goose), leveret (young hare) and capon (young rooster) but also badger and even cat on it as well! They even had 'live pies' – huge pastries filled with living frogs or birds! Dessert could be jellies, cream, egg custard, strawberries, pears poached in a rich sauce of wine, cinnamon, sugar, ginger and saffron or plums stewed in rose-water. Their banquets had loads of courses and went on for hours.

Poor people couldn't afford meat and usually ate a type of stew called *pottage* (made with vegetables like leeks, onions, beans, peas and kale, flavoured with various herbs). They drank ale, mead (a drink made with honey) and cider – only the rich could afford wine as grapes didn't grow well in Ireland and had to be imported. The bread they ate was cheap corn or rye bread that often had pieces of grit in it that wore down their teeth. That's when things were going well and they *had* bread. Famines were a common and dreaded occurrence when the crops failed and there was a bad harvest.

In 1317, not only was there a famine throughout Europe, but an army led by Scottish nobleman Edward Bruce stole, burned and pillaged its way round Ireland. It's said that starving Irish people started eating each other! No wonder Edward was soon killed at the Battle of Faughart. Parts of his body were sent to the four corners of Ireland and his head to the English king.

There was another bad famine in Co. Dublin in 1331, but that summer a pod of 200 whales washed up at the mouth of the river Dodder. The starving poor were treated to as much whale meat as they could eat.

Some people who lived in towns had fruit and vegetable gardens and made their own cheese and butter from cow or goat's milk. Others kept beehives to produce honey to flavour bland foods and to make their own mead. They were allowed to fish if they lived near rivers, lakes or the sea, but could not fish in a castle moat. The fish in that were for nobles in the castle only!

The native Irish who lived in the countryside and mountains kept cattle and farmed and foraged for wild foods like fruit, berries, nuts and mushrooms. They generally weren't bothered by the Normans who kept close to their castles and towns. So the Irish were mostly free to do what they wanted. Mostly.

Here's a couple of medieval recipes you can try for yourself. No whales, pottage, jellied eels or live pies in sight. Just something that might *spike* your interest ...

A DEADLY! MEDIEVAL COOKBOOK

ROAST HEDGEHOG

Here's a real medieval recipe for roast hedgehog: *'Hedgehog should have its throat cut, be singed and gutted, then trussed like a pullet, then pressed in a towel until very dry; and then roast it and eat with cameline sauce, or in pastry with wild duck sauce. Note that if the hedgehog refuses to unroll, put it in hot water, and then it will straighten itself.'*

Hedgehogs are now an endangered protected species, which means you can't just go out and hunt one with your bow and arrow. But if your dad squishes one in his car on a country road, then ... maybe the recipe on the next page is one for you. Or maybe not!

Serves 5–6

1–2 tbsp vegetable oil
400g of hedgehog, skinned, gutted and cut into bite-size chunks
1 onion
1 green pepper
1 carrot
1 turnip
2 tomatoes
2.5 cm piece of fresh ginger, finely sliced
300 ml water
1 tsp salt

1) Roughly chop all the vegetables.
2) Heat the oil in a pan and fry the hedgehog meat for 1–2 minutes.
3) Transfer the hedgehog to a large casserole dish and add the other ingredients.
4) Bring to the boil then cover and simmer on a low heat for an hour or until the meat is tender.

Hey, don't worry if you can't get hold of road-killed hedgehog. Just replace it with lamb or beef chunks.

LECHE LOMBARD

Rich medieval households ate a dessert called *Leche Lombard*, which was a dish consisting of pork, eggs, pepper, cloves, currants, dates and sugar boiled together in a pig's bladder, then sliced and served in a rich sauce. Because we don't use meat in desserts in modern times, here's a yummy recipe for Leche Lombard you can make without it.

Serves 4

270 ml of runny honey
225 g chopped almonds
270 g breadcrumbs
½ tsp cinnamon
½ tsp ginger
Pinch of nutmeg
1 tsp of ginger mixed with 1 tsp of sugar for the topping

1) Add the cinnamon, ginger and nutmeg to the honey and simmer gently in a pan for 10 minutes.
2) Stir in the almonds and breadcrumbs. Cook for another few minutes until the mixture sticks together.
3) Allow to cool on waxed paper and mould into an oblong roll.
4) Sprinkle the sugar and ginger mixture over the top.

Meet Hugh, who works as a spit-boy* in a busy castle kitchen. He may spin the handle of a spit all day but does he also spin tall tales? **Answers below.**

A) RICH PEOPLE THOUGHT VEGETABLES WERE ONLY FIT TO FEED THE POOR.

C) THE FOOD NOBLES EAT ISN'T VERY SPICY.

B) POOR PEOPLE ARE ALLOWED TO HUNT DEER, BOAR, HARES AND RABBITS.

D) PEOPLE OFTEN EAT OFF A PLATE MADE OF STALE BREAD.

ANSWERS: Hugh told porky pies a couple of times. a) True. The only vegetables nobles ate were garlic, leeks and onions. Because of their rich diets and a lack of fibre and vitamins, they had loads of health problems. b) Nope! Only nobles were allowed to hunt. If a poor person was caught poaching, they could have their hands cut off! c) False. Knights brought back expensive spices like pepper, cinnamon, cloves, turmeric and mustard from their Crusades in the Middle East. Rich people liked spicy food. d) True. These were called trenchers, and after you'd eaten off the trencher, you could eat it!

* See page 53.

BLEEDING GOOD HUMOUR

MEDIEVAL MEDICINE

In medieval times, many people became ill due to poor hygiene, and often people were wounded in some dangerous escapade. There were no police, and violence – and perhaps death – was just one insult away!

Today, doctors know how to treat injuries and disease, but back then some of the methods of treating the sick and wounded can only be described as **DEADLY!**

TWAK!
... BUT YOUR HEAD!
OWWW!
EACH PART OF THE BODY IS UNDER THE INFLUENCE OF A SIGN OF THE ZODIAC!
ZODIAC MAN
ARIES
TAURUS
LEO
ALSO, YOUR BODY HAS FOUR LIQUIDS CALLED HUMOURS. WHEN THESE ARE EQUAL, YOU'RE HEALTHY.
WARM & DRY
YELLOW BILE
SUMMER
FIRE
AIR
SPRING
BLOOD
WATER
EARTH
WINTER
PHLEGM
AUTUMN
BLACK BILE
COLD & DRY
WHEN THEY'RE OUT OF BALANCE, YOU'RE SICK. AND I CAN TELL YOU'RE SICK! VERY, VERY, SICK!
BUT IT'S JUST MY ELBOW. IT HURTS SOMETIMES WHEN I --
NONSENSE! YOUR BLOOD IS ALL OUT OF WHACK!
YOU NEED LEECHES TO SUCK THE BAD BLOOD OUT OF YOUR HEAD!

Yes, that's right. When he wasn't pulling out teeth or cutting off an infected arm, the *barber surgeon* could give you a nice short back and sides. The red-and-white striped pole outside a modern barber shop harks back to the days of barber surgeons, with the red symbolising blood and the white symbolising bandages.

Barber surgeons had businesses within the walls of the Norman towns in Ireland. If you couldn't afford to go to one (yes – people actually paid for these 'treatments'), or you lived in the countryside, as most Irish people did, you could go and see the local *bean feasa* (woman of knowledge) or *bean leighis* (woman of healing).

These women had knowledge of the healing power of certain plants and herbs and knew how to cure warts, sore throats, backache and other minor ailments. They acted as midwives who helped women through childbirth. They also had knowledge of the supernatural and a lot of their cures involved incantations and spells. In later years, some of these women were accused of being witches.

All in all, there were some pretty nasty diseases lurking around medieval Ireland that modern medicine has pretty much taken care of. One of these diseases was called leprosy – a contagious condition that affects the skin and had no known cure. The only way to control the spread was to lock up the poor sufferers in special leper hospitals, one of which was built near St Stephen's Green in Dublin. This was then moved out to the foot of the Dublin Mountains and was called Baile na Lobhar which means *Town of the Lepers*. Nowadays, it's known as Leopardstown and there's a famous racecourse there.

This is Molly, a bean leighis, known for her incredible healing skills, but there's no cure for being a liar. Does she speak the truth or just a load of old codswallop? **Answers below.**

A) MY CURE FOR A SORE THROAT IS A NECKLACE OF WORMS.

D) A SPRIG OF MINT OR LAVENDER TIED AROUND YOUR WRIST WILL FIX AN UPSET TUMMY.

B) I RUB THE BLOOD OF AN EEL ON WARTS TO GET RID OF THEM.

E) IF A WHOLE HOUSEHOLD HAS BEEN AFFLICTED BY AN INFECTIOUS DISEASE, PUT SOME SHEEP INTO THE HOUSE FOR THREE DAYS.

C) TO CURE ARTHRITIS, WHIP THE AFFLICTED JOINTS WITH NETTLES.

ANSWERS: Although she has some wacky cures, Molly's not lying and believes her medicines will work. a) Whether it was effective is another matter! b) Uh-huh. Gross but true. Again, not sure if this worked! c) True. Painful as this sounds, it was thought that nettles had healing properties. d) Yes, healers recommended this. e) Yes Mad, but yes! I wouldn't like to be the one to clean up all the sheep dung afterwards!

All over Ireland skulls have been found from the medieval period by archaeologists that had small, circular holes in them (the skulls, not the archaeologists). This was likely done by medieval doctors who believed they were helping patients with head injuries or severe headaches. Perhaps they thought they were relieving pressure or releasing evil spirits, but this method of surgery – called **trepanation** – was practised all over the ancient world.

The fact that some skulls showed evidence of healing means that the patients survived, but your guess is as good as mine as to whether this scary procedure actually worked. However, one story goes that after a young Irish chieftain named Cenn Fáelad mac Ailella received a serious head wound, some monks performed a trepanation on him. Cenn Fáelad not only made a full recovery, but started remembering *everything* he was ever told. Could be pretty handy come exam time!

In 1348, another invader crept into Ireland, this time uninvited. It landed in towns and devastated the mostly Norman population there. You couldn't see it or hear it, but its effects were horrific. This time, it was carried by fleas on the backs of rats that had sneaked into the bellies of ships coming from Europe. This was the terrible disease called the Black Death.

It was given this name because when an infected rat flea bit you, horrible black boils filled with pus formed on your body. Usually within a few days you died a terrible, agonising death. Few who got it survived and it tore through the Irish towns like a dreadful whirlwind, sometimes claiming many members of the same family at the same time.

Once a household was known to have caught it, a big white 'X' was painted on their door and they had to stay inside. So many people died that coffins couldn't be made quickly enough and 'plague pits' had to be dug where lots of people could be buried at once.

Brave (or stupid!) men called carters gathered up the dead to take them for burial. These carters were terribly at risk of catching the disease themselves, but they were likely very well paid!

The Irish population, who lived in the countryside and in the mountains, were mostly unaffected by it, probably because rats prefer towns, where there's plenty of food. Medieval doctors didn't know that rat fleas caused the Black Death (also known as **bubonic plague**) as lice and fleas were an everyday problem for people living in medieval times. They thought it was caused by 'corrupted airs'. Up to half the population died. Ordinary people feared it was a punishment sent by God or that it was the End of the World. Although the Irish wouldn't have wished such a horrible death even on their worst enemy, the Black Death did have the effect of driving a lot of the Norman barons out of their castles and back to England and Wales.

FAMOUS IRISH CASTLES #4*

BIRR CASTLE CO. OFFALY
4

CENTURY BUILT: 12TH
HAUNTED: 0
DEADLINESS: 8

The castle is a family home but it has gardens open to the public. The world's tallest box hedge (12 metres) grows here. Ireland's Historic Science Centre is also on the grounds. In 1869, the world's first road death occurred near the castle when a woman fell out of a steam-powered car and was killed.

DUBLIN CASTLE CO. DUBLIN
17

CENTURY BUILT: 13TH
HAUNTED: 0
DEADLINESS: 5

The castle was built on the site of a Viking settlement beside the dark pool ('Dubh Linn') which gives Dublin its name. A castle has been here since the days of King John and was the headquarters of British administration in Ireland until Ireland's independence in 1922. The author of Dracula, Bram Stoker, worked in Dublin Castle from 1866 to 1878.

BLACKROCK CASTLE CO. CORK
5

CENTURY BUILT: 16TH
HAUNTED: 0
DEADLINESS: 6

Home to a planetarium, this castle was built on the orders of Queen Elizabeth I to repel pirates and other invaders. The castle is the oldest structure still in use in Cork city and has been a court, a lighthouse, a signalling station and a gun battery. It was twice destroyed by fire.

BAGENAL'S CASTLE CO. DOWN
2

CENTURY BUILT: 16TH
HAUNTED: 0
DEADLINESS: 5

Built on the site of a 12th-century abbey by Sir Nicholas Bagenal, an English settler, this fortified house was surrounded by a bawn and had an orchard and garden. Nicholas Bagenal's arch-nemesis, Hugh O'Neill, married Nicholas's sister Mabel, probably just to annoy him. The castle now houses the Newry and Mourne Museum.

DALKEY CASTLE CO. DUBLIN

(15)

CENTURY BUILT: 14TH
HAUNTED: 0
DEADLINESS: 5

Dalkey Castle, also known as Goat Castle, was just one of seven fortified town houses built to store the goods that were off-loaded in Dalkey, the main port for Dublin in medieval times. It is home to a travel-back-in-time heritage centre. Dalkey may have been one of the ports where the Black Death entered into Ireland in 1348.

CASHEL CASTLE CO. TIPPERARY

(11)

CENTURY BUILT: 4TH
HAUNTED: 🎭🎭🎭
DEADLINESS: 8

The Rock of Cashel was the seat of the High Kings of Munster and a fort has been on the site for at least 1,600 years. Legend says that Saint Patrick banished the Devil from a cave 30 km away. Satan was so annoyed that he bit off a chunk of mountain and broke a tooth. Where the tooth landed formed the Rock of Cashel. In 1647, the Earl of Inchquin burned 800 people to death in the cathedral there. A room called the Vicar's Choral Quarters is said to be haunted, and the sound of a ghostly coach and horses can often be heard.

ROCKFLEET CASTLE CO. MAYO

(35)

CENTURY FIRST BUILT: 16TH
HAUNTED: 0
DEADLINESS: 6

This lonely tower house belonged to the family of the famous Pirate Queen, Grace O'Malley (Granuaile), who died here at a ripe old age. It is said that all of the castle's treasure is buried in the surrounding hills, and anyone who digs it up will be met by the Dullahan — a headless horseman!

ROSS CASTLE CO. KERRY

(36)

CENTURY BUILT: 15TH
HAUNTED: 🎭🎭
DEADLINESS: 7

This castle was built by the cruel English Lord Richard Nugent, nicknamed the Black Baron, who once hanged a poor beggar just for stealing a loaf of bread. It turned out it was a dog who'd stolen it. His daughter, Sabina, locked herself in the castle and starved to death after her boyfriend Orwin — who was the son of her father's enemy — was drowned rowing across Lough Sheelin in a storm. Sabina's ghost and the ghost of her father are said to haunt the castle.

* See map, page 138.

WINDING DOWN
FUN AND LEISURE

It might sound like it was all doom and gloom back in medieval times. To be sure, life was tougher than it is today but that doesn't mean both the Irish and the Normans didn't have a laugh as well. In fact, people had about eight weeks' worth of holidays and festivals a year, which is more than the average person gets now! Big celebrations took place during Easter, Christmas, May Day, after the ploughing of the fields, and at the end of the harvest.

Lots of the games and pastimes were more or less the same as the ones you might know now: hide 'n' seek, tag (or tig), swimming, fishing, blind man's bluff, hopscotch, conkers, chess, draughts, card games, marbles, camogie and hurling. But have you heard of **queek**? What about **chevy chase**, a game that King Edward III banned? A game of **knucklebones**, anyone? Here's how these games were played. Maybe you and your friends can help bring them back into fashion!

Queek – You need a large checkered cloth of two colours as a board. If you don't have one, you can draw out a board with chalk, so long as there are two different colours. Each person takes turns tossing a pebble. But before the pebble lands they must say out loud what colour they think the pebble will land on. The first person to guess right ten times wins.

Chevy chase – You need an even number of players – minimum of ten – and a large play area to play chevy chase. Divide the group into two teams and go to opposite ends of the play area. Each team then draws a large square (with chalk or rope) at their end of the play area – this is the 'prison cell'. One person from each team is chosen (or volunteers) to be the other team's prisoner and goes into their cell. Each team chooses someone to rescue their imprisoned team member and to bring him or her back without being caught (or tagged). If that person makes it to the prison without being tagged, then the goal is to wait and choose a moment for both to try to run back to their team's side without getting recaptured

If the team member is caught by the opposing team, they also become a prisoner needing rescue. So each team is kept busy by trying both to rescue their own prisoners and to prevent the prisoners from the opposite side from being rescued! At the end of a time limit, the team with the most 'prisoners' wins. Or you can play until one team has captured all the opposing team's members.

Knucklebones — This gruesome-sounding game was played with actual knucklebones, but you can use five pebbles instead. Draw your own cool designs (like skulls or flowers) on them with markers. (I'm still gonna call them 'knucklebones' or 'bones' though!) You can play with other people or just by yourself.

To decide who goes first, each player takes turns tossing all five of the knucklebones at once to see how many he or she can catch on the back of their hand before they fall. The player who catches the most bones goes first.

To start the game, toss all the bones onto a smooth, flat surface such as a floor or table. Toss one bone into the air. With that same hand, pick up one of the bones lying on the table. Catch the bone that was tossed in the air before it falls to the table.

Continue to toss and pick up bones, one by one. Put them aside until they've all been gathered.

Toss and pick up bones by twos, threes, fours and so on, until you toss and gather all the bones at once. If the tossed knucklebone falls before you complete your move, you lose your turn and the next player gets to go. The player who picks up all of the knucklebones first is the winner.

Jesters or fools were hired by kings and wealthy nobles for entertainment at parties and festivals. There were different types of jesters in medieval Ireland.

DRÚTH – a performer of physical comedy and vocal antics.

FUIRSEOIR – a mimic and contortionist, able to twist his body into weird positions.

CREACAIRE – scares the wits out of the audience with loud noises and sudden jumps.

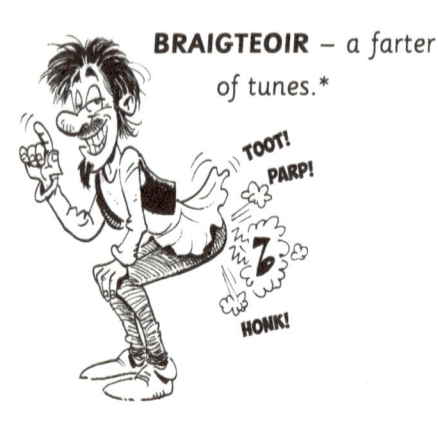

BRAIGTEOIR – a farter of tunes.*

* See page 54 for a career opportunity in this profession.

Norman nobles often held contests around festival times called **tourneys**, where they could show off their warrior skills. Here they took part in mock battles called **melees**, where two groups of knights would fight each other. They held archery competitions and also **jousted**, where two knights on horseback ran at each other and each tried to knock the other knight out of his saddle using a blunted lance. These 'friendly' games often ended with serious injury or even death!

Nobles also loved the sport of **hawking**, and Irish hawks were highly prized. For once, Gerald of Wales told the truth.

The sport did not arrive with the Normans – there's mention of it in tales about Fionn Mac Cumhaill and his legendary Fianna warriors.*

> IRELAND PRODUCES HAWKS, FALCONS AND SPARROWHAWKS ABUNDANTLY... MOST SUITABLE FOR CATCHING THEIR PREY AND ALL TO AFFORD AMUSEMENT TO THE NOBLES.

> I KNOW WHAT IT IS BUT HE'S THE BARON'S SON AND HE CAN HAVE WHAT HE LIKES!

* See Deadly! Irish History – The Celts

One of the earliest games of **football** was played in Ireland. I don't mean they played a game at six o'clock in the morning, I mean a game was played back in the summer of 1308. Football wasn't like it is now as there could have been dozens of players and the goals several miles apart. It was a lot more violent too – no one threw themselves on the grass looking for a free kick. In fact, it's reported that at that game in 1308, a man called John McCrocan accidentally stabbed his friend, William Bernard, when they both went for the ball. Thankfully, there are now rules against carrying knives into matches.

WELL THAT'S THE GAME OVER, THEN!

The ball itself was made from an inflated pig's bladder. In later years, the bladder was covered in leather to make it last longer. The idea was to keep the ball in the air for as long as possible by punching and kicking it.

Some entertainments were cruel by our modern standards but were enjoyed by many people back in medieval times. Sports such as **cockfighting** and **bullbaiting** involved animals fighting each other to the death, with bets placed on the outcome. Even the **hanging of criminals** attracted large crowds. It was like going to the cinema for them! It's not so much that people were more evil back then, it's just that life was much tougher and shorter and death was never far away. They also didn't see animals as having any rights at all and they certainly wouldn't have thought most animals had feelings.

ISOBEL, HUGH AND FIONNTÁN

MEDIEVAL KIDS

It wasn't easy being a kid back in medieval times, though it was easier for some than others. Isobel, aged ten, is the youngest daughter of the Norman baron who owns the castle. Hugh, aged twelve, works hard in the castle kitchen. Fionntán, aged eleven, is an Irish lad who lives out in the countryside near the castle. Let's see what happens when their paths cross ...

Isobel's Diary: Oh, I do hope those awful workmen finish the chapel roof soon! I was awoken by their loathsome sawing and hammering shortly after sunrise. I complained to Father, but he just wants his castle to be finished before the workmen stop for the winter so he doesn't care a jot about MY feelings. 'Just one more month, my dear Isobel,' he says. It's all right for him — he sleeps on the other side of the Keep, away from all the horrible noise. Sometimes I think I am utterly invisible!

Hugh's Diary: Cook wanted all the scullions in the kitchen very early this morn 'cos his lordship has guests staying and we have to get the fires ready to cook their breakfast. So I've been up since three hour 'fore sunrise, fetching water from the well and splittin' logs. I got a splinter but I don't have time to look at it. It's sore but it'll work its own way out, I suppose.

Fionntán's Diary: One of the cows strayed last night and I've been sent by my aite* to fetch it. That's all right — I like being away by myself and I'm good at tracking. Not that it would take an expert to track this beast — she's left a trail in the grass a blind man could follow. Looks like she's heading towards the castle. The sun's just come up so I'd better get a move on as I don't want to run into any Sasanaigh.**

* Foster father. Many Irish kids were sent to live with another family until they were teenagers. See *Deadly! Irish History – The Celts*.
** What the Irish called the Normans.

I: One good thing about the chapel not being finished yet is that I don't have to go to mass every single morning! The priest says mass in Latin and I only understand the odd word, so it's really boring. After breakfast, Father went out hawking with his friends who are staying with us. They are very impressed with Father's new castle. They should be as building started on it before I was born. Mother is showing the lady guests around the place, so she has no time for me. I went down to the stables to talk to the horses. They seem to be the only ones who listen to me these days.

H: Cook doesn't usually shout at us scullions much, but he did this morn. His round face was all red and puffed up and he were waving his fat arms around like a windmill. If he ain't careful, he'll keel over dead. It's all 'cos he wants to show off his cooking to the guests. Me and Davey and Richard had a good laugh making faces behind his back but he caught me at it and gave me a good kick up the backside and told me to get out of his sight. I went down to the stables to look at the horses till he calmed down.

F: *How fast can a cow go? I've seen them run but they never run far so this one must have had extra grass for breakfast! I'd been following her trail for a good hour before I finally found her not far from the castle. I hadn't ever been this close to it – we always avoid it. I've never seen anything as big, except for a mountain. The white walls reflected the sun so much it hurt my eyes, and the flags on the towers flapped proudly in the wind. What kind of people live in a place like this? My aite would say the wrong kind. He says that they have strange ways and that they'd kill you as soon as look at you. They can't all be bad ... can they?*

I: I saw one of those horrid kitchen scullions in the stables. I know he's not allowed in there and he knew it too because he hid. I pretended not to notice him because in truth I am a little afraid of the scullions. They're always so dirty and uncouth. I quickly saddled one of the mares — Daisy — and took her out the gate. The gatesman asked me where I was going. I lied and told him I was going to join Father out hawking and he allowed me to pass. He isn't the sharpest sword in the scabbard — doesn't he know little girls don't go hawking?

H: I thought there'd be no one in the stables 'cos I'd heard they'd all gone a-hawkin', but there she was, his lordship's littlest daughter. Isobel, I think she be called. I hid when I seen her so I don't think she noticed me. I watched her saddlin' a grey mare, but it didn't look to me like she done it right. Richard's brother Roland works in the stables and he showed me how it's done one time when we was playin' knucklebones. But off she went out the front gate and across the drawbridge, bold as brass.

F: I know I was told not to go near the castle but I didn't know when I'd get another chance to see it. It looked like it was from another world and had plonked itself right in the middle of our land. I heard the drum of hoofbeats behind me and turned to see a girl about my age in fine red clothes riding a grey horse that looked too big for her. She looked like she was just as shocked to see me!

I: Oh my days! When I saw that savage Irish boy riding on a cow, I thought I might die there on the spot! I didn't think it possible to be scruffier than a scullion, but there he was — all wild-haired and barefoot! Daisy whinnied and reared up on her hind legs. The saddle strap must have come undone because I fell to the ground.

H: When I saw Lady Isobel had gone off with the saddle all wrong, I snuck out through the sally port and went through the village after her for I were afraid she might do herself a mischief. I ran as fast as me legs could turn and spotted her grey horse and her red dress against the green grass away down the valley. I also seen somebody in yellow riding on a dun cow. It's mostly the Irish who wear yellow! I run and run till me lungs was fit to burst!

F: That leather and wood thing the Sasanaigh put on their horses* slid off and the girl went crashing to the ground. I heard a crack and she let out such a screech I nearly turned and ran. But I could see from the weird shape her arm was twisted in that she'd broken it.

* The Irish didn't saddle their horses.

I: I was terrified of the wild Irish boy, but even though I couldn't understand what he was saying, I knew he wasn't trying to hurt me. Gently as he could, he set my arm straight — it was really sore. Then he found two tree branches and carefully tied them either side of my arm with some tassels from his own cloak.

H: As I got closer, I saw an Irish lad bent over Lady Isobel and I were about to kick him in the head. But Lady Isobel cried out, 'No, stop! He's helping me!' and I could see that he was. He'd fixed her arm up, good and proper. He made gestures for me to take off my mantle and he used it to make a sling. Where'd he learn to do that?

F: My Aunt Molly is a bean leighis* and she showed me how to set a broken arm. She said I might need to know one day. I was nervous I might hurt the girl but I think I did OK.

---

* A healing woman. See page 94.

I: The scullion — who said his name was Hugh — put Daisy's saddle back on. Properly this time. He helped me mount her then led us back towards the castle. We waved goodbye to the Irish boy who said his name was Funtone (the Irish have such funny names!). I have learnt never to judge a person by how they look, even people as scruffy as those two! We met Father and his friends as they returned from hawking. Father was most upset to see I had broken my arm, but after I explained Funtone and Hugh had helped me, he calmed down.

H: I thought mayhaps his Lordship might skelp me or worse, for us scullions ain't allowed to even look at, never mind touch, nobles. But after Lady Isobel explained all, he were right nice to me. He even patted me on the head. I saw him wipe his hand after, but still!

F: My aite was right — the Sasanaigh are a bit strange. But they're still human.

FAMOUS IRISH CASTLES #5*

CLOGH OUGHTER CASTLE CO. CAVAN

13

CENTURY BUILT: 13TH
HAUNTED: 0
DEADLINESS: 6

Built on a tiny island in the middle of a lough, this small round castle can only be accessed by boat. The island may have been the site of an ancient crannóg**. The castle was the last place to hold out against Oliver Cromwell's English army in 1653. Several skeletons have been found there.

BALLYGALLY CASTLE CO. ANTRIM

3

CENTURY BUILT: 17TH
HAUNTED: 🌣🌣🌣
DEADLINESS: 7

Now a hotel, this castle is thought to be one of the most haunted in Ireland. It has at least two ghosts: Lady Isobel who knocks on guests' doors at night, and a Madam Nixon who can be heard walking around the hotel in her silk dress. Lady Isobel Shaw fell to her death when she tried to escape from a room her husband had locked her in.

GREENCASTLE CO. DOWN

24

CENTURY BUILT: 13TH
HAUNTED: 🌣
DEADLINESS: 5

Built by the Norman knight Hugh de Lacy at the same time as Carlingford Castle (page 40) which is directly across Carlingford Lough, the pair of castles guarded the narrow entry to the lough. The bones of a woman and a child, dating from the time the castle was built, were found here in 2003.

TULLY CASTLE CO. FERMANAGH

39

CENTURY BUILT: 17TH
HAUNTED: 🌣🌣🌣🌣
DEADLINESS: 8

Built on a hill by the shores of Lough Erne, this T-shaped fortified house has the shortest and bloodiest history of any castle in Ireland. It was lived in for just over twenty years until there was a massacre here on Christmas Day of 1641. The Maguire family killed 60 women and children and 15 men. The ghosts of the murdered people are said to return on Christmas Day every year.

* See map, page 138.

** An artificial island. See page 11 and also see *Deadly! Irish History: The Celts* book.

ENNISKILLEN CASTLE CO. FERMANAGH

21

CENTURY BUILT: 16TH
HAUNTED: 💀
DEADLINESS: 6

The first castle was built here by the Irish warlord, Hugh Maguire, but soon fell into English hands. Then Irish hands. Then English hands again. The castle is now home to the Fermanagh County Museum. The ghost of a soldier is often seen patrolling near the north gate of the castle.

TRIM CASTLE CO. MEATH

38

CENTURY BUILT: 12TH
HAUNTED: 💀💀💀
DEADLINESS: 7

The largest castle in Ireland, with a keep of unusual design – it has twenty sides! It also has lots of secret passages and rooms, some of which are said to be haunted. It has appeared in a few famous movies. The ghost of a woman laying gold coins on a cloth has been spotted many times.

HUNTINGTON CASTLE CO. CARLOW

25

CENTURY BUILT: 17TH
HAUNTED: 💀💀💀💀
DEADLINESS: 7

The original three-storey fortified tower house was built by Baron Esmonde. In the basement there is an ancient well dating back to the days of the druids. The ghost of a soldier shot by mistake by his own side is said to knock on the castle door. And the pirate queen Grace O'Malley's granddaughter Ailish's ghost is said to haunt here, combing her hair and crying. A group of ghostly monks have also been seen walking the grounds.

LEAP CASTLE CO. OFFALY

31

CENTURY BUILT: 13TH
HAUNTED: 💀💀💀💀
DEADLINESS: 10

Home to the ruthless O'Carroll clan, this spooky castle is one of the most haunted ever. Here's just a few of the ghosts said to roam its dark depths: a Red Lady who wanders the halls with a dagger. The spirits of two little girls run up and down the stairs. There's also a demon simply called 'It'. In the 1900s, workers discovered an oubliette*** behind a wall. There they found human skeletons impaled on spikes. Visit, if you dare!

*** See pages 29 and 133.

SÉAMUS THE SINISTER SWORDSMAN

Loads of cool stuff from the medieval era has been found by archaeologists over the years and the finds are now displayed in Irish museums. See if you can find these things in this tale about *Séamus the Sinister Swordsman*.

Séamus the Sinister Swordsman

The castle of Norman Baron, Sir Richard Le Mal—

Sir Richard, my name is **Finbar**.

My squire said you had **important information**, Irish man. Make it **quick!**

What if I told you I knew where **King Conn** was going to be tomorrow... so you could capture him and hold him for **ransom?**

King Conn? My greatest Irish **enemy?** I'm **interested!** But how did you come by this information, Finbar?

Because...

KRA-KOM!!

...I'm King Conn's **Tánaiste!***

* SECOND-IN-COMMAND

NEXT DAY--
BLESS YOU, KING CONN AND LADY MAEVE! BLESS YOU FOR GIVING ALL THIS FOOD TO THE LEPER HOSPITAL!*
NOT AT ALL, FATHER. WE'LL BE BACK IN A FEW WEEKS WITH MORE!
STAY OUT! DANGER!
LEPER HOSPITAL
*SEE PAGE 93.
I FEEL SO SORRY FOR ALL THOSE POOR PEOPLE WITH LEPROSY, DAD.
AYE - ME TOO, MAEVE. WE MUST DO ALL WE CAN TO HELP THOSE LESS FORTUNATE THAN OURSELVES.
STOP RIGHT WHERE YOU ARE, KING CONN!
SIR RICHARD'S MEN!!
PLEASE - JUST TAKE ME! LEAVE MY DAUGHTER ALONE!
DON'T WORRY - IT'S JUST YOU WE WANT! BESIDES, WE HAVE TO GIVE HER THE RANSOM DEMAND!

LATER, AT KING CONN'S STRONGHOLD--
... AND THEY TOOK DAD TO SIR RICHARD'S CASTLE AND GAVE ME THIS!
3,000 CATTLE! PLUS 10,000 SILVER COINS?! WE CAN'T PAY THIS - IT'S OUTRAGEOUS!
BUT WE HAVE TO TRY! WE HAVE TO!
MAEVE, MAEVE, MAEVE - WE SIMPLY HAVEN'T GOT IT! IF WE HAD, BELIEVE ME, I'D HAPPILY PAY IT. AS TÁNAISTE, I WILL NOW ...
THEN WE MUST TRY AND BREAK DAD OUT OF THE CASTLE!
HA HA HA HA! YES, LET'S JUST WALK UP TO SIR RICHARD'S FRONT DOOR AND ASK HIM NICELY IF HE'LL LET KING CONN GO!
HA HA HA!
I WILL DO IT, LADY MAEVE ...

... IF YOU'LL LET ME.
HA HA HA HA HA! SÉAMUS?!? YEAH - LET'S SEND SÉAMUS TO RESCUE KING CONN! THAT'LL WORK!
HA HA HA!
SÉAMUS THE SINISTER SWORDSMAN!
HA HA! HOO HOO HOO!
HA HA HA!
PAY NO ATTENTION TO HIM, SÉAMUS. YOU'RE BRAVER THAN ALL THESE MEN PUT TOGETHER.
COME ON, SÉAMUS! WE HAVE PLANS TO MAKE!
FIRST ORDER OF BUSINESS WHEN I'M MADE KING ...
... GET RID OF PLUCKY LITTLE MAEVE!

At Sir Richard's castle--

Well, King Conn...

...I do hope you find your prison tower *nice* and *uncomfortable* and much to your *disliking!*

How did you know where to *find* me, you rat?!?

Your Tánaiste, Finbar, paid me a visit. He's a *cunning one*, all right!

That wee *weasel!* When I get out of here, I'll...

You *won't* be getting out of here. It was Finbar who suggested I set an unreasonably *high* ransom...

When you don't return, *he* will be made king. Then he and I can enjoy *carving up* your little kingdom!

...and he *won't* be planning a *rescue!*

AT MAEVE'S HOUSE--
TO GET YOU INSIDE THE CASTLE, YOU'RE GOING TO HAVE TO LOOK LIKE A NORMAN, SÉAMUS!
SO THAT MEANS A NORMAN HAIRCUT ...
WHOO!
SNIP SNIPPITY SNIP SNIP!
... AND A NORMAN OUTFIT!
WELL, TURN AROUND WHILE I GET CHANGED - I'M SHY!
I LOOK LIKE A RIGHT EEJIT!
MAYBE - BUT YOU'D PASS FOR A NORMAN! LET'S GET GOING TO THE CASTLE!

BACK AT THE CASTLE--
THIS IS AS FAR AS I CAN GO, SEAMUS! REMEMBER OUR PLAN!
NOW PLEASE BRING BACK MY FATHER!
PECK!
BLUSH!
I DON'T KNOW WHETHER I'M BEING BRAVE OR STUPID ...
... BUT EITHER WAY I HAVE TO TRY AND SAVE KING CONN!
HALT, STRANGER! STATE YOUR BUSINESS!
I'VE GOT SOME NICE CHEESE FOR SIR RICHARD'S TABLE!
PHWOARR! THAT REEKS! GET IT AWAY FROM ME!
PONG!
WHIFF!

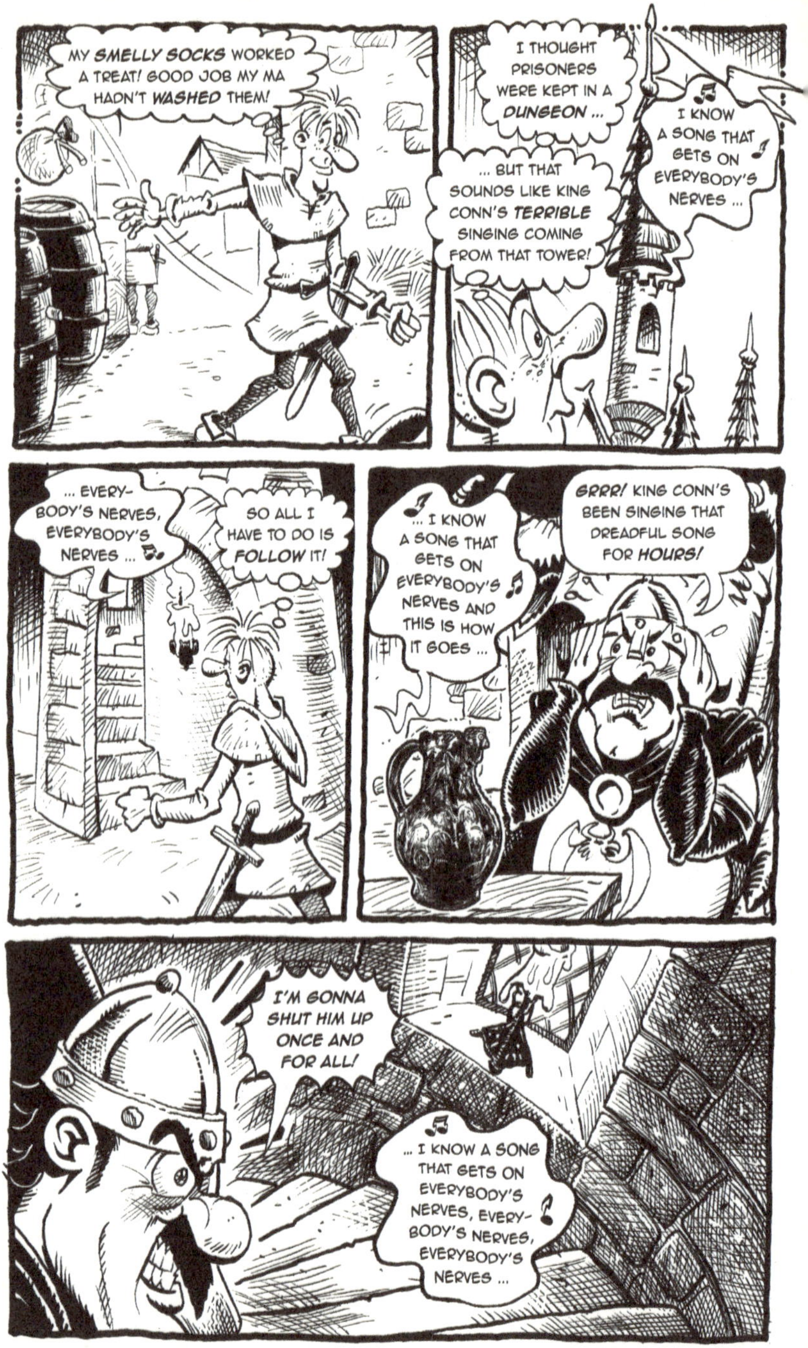
MY SMELLY SOCKS WORKED A TREAT! GOOD JOB MY MA HADN'T WASHED THEM!
I THOUGHT PRISONERS WERE KEPT IN A DUNGEON ...
... BUT THAT SOUNDS LIKE KING CONN'S TERRIBLE SINGING COMING FROM THAT TOWER!
I KNOW A SONG THAT GETS ON EVERYBODY'S NERVES ...
... EVERY-BODY'S NERVES, EVERYBODY'S NERVES ...
SO ALL I HAVE TO DO IS FOLLOW IT!
... I KNOW A SONG THAT GETS ON EVERYBODY'S NERVES AND THIS IS HOW IT GOES ...
GRRR! KING CONN'S BEEN SINGING THAT DREADFUL SONG FOR HOURS!
I'M GONNA SHUT HIM UP ONCE AND FOR ALL!
... I KNOW A SONG THAT GETS ON EVERYBODY'S NERVES, EVERY-BODY'S NERVES, EVERYBODY'S NERVES ...

OOH! ER ... UM ... HELLO!
... I KNOW A SONG THAT GETS ON EVERYBODY'S NERVES AND THIS IS HOW IT GOES ...
WHO THE - ?!? YOU'RE NOT ONE OF MY MEN!
YOU HAVE NO CHANCE AGAINST ME, SCOUNDREL!
THESE STAIRS GO CLOCKWISE SO THAT RIGHT-HANDED ATTACKERS CANNOT SWING THEIR SWORDS!
GOOD JOB I'M LEFT-HANDED,* THEN!*
GULP!
*SO THAT EXPLAINS SÉAMUS'S NICKNAME! 'SINISTER' IS THE LATIN WORD FOR 'LEFT-HANDED'.
I'M OFF!
COME BACK HERE, YOU CHICKEN!
WAHH!
TRIP!
I KNOW A SONG THAT GETS ON EVERYBODY'S NERVES ...

... EVERYBODY'S NERV- HUHP!P SEAMUS, IS THAT YOU?
ERKK!
INDEED IT IS, SIRE! NOW, SIR RICHARD, GIVE ME THE KEY TO RELEASE MY KING!
AT LEAST HE'S STOPPED THAT TERRIBLE SINGING!
YOU'LL NEVER MAKE IT OUT OF HERE! MY MEN ARE ALL OVER THIS CASTLE!
YOU PUT A LOT OF FAITH IN MEN WHO ARE FOOLED BY A BAG OF SWEATY SOCKS! BESIDES ...
... WE'RE NOT GONNA BE IN THE CASTLE!
YOU FOUND HIM! I KNEW YOU COULD DO IT, SEAMUS!
HE'S QUITE THE BRAVE WARRIOR, MAEVE!
HE CERTAINLY IS!
BLUSH!
AHH, IT WAS NOTHIN'!

DID YOU FIND ALL THE OBJECTS FROM THE MUSEUMS? ANSWERS ON PAGE 144.

VISITING A CASTLE RUIN

Most castles in Ireland are in ruins, but you can still open a door to the past if you use a little imagination. When you visit a ruin, keep an eye out for these things:

1) MOAT: A dry, grassy ditch that surrounds the castle, which was usually filled with water as part of the castle's defences.

2) GATEHOUSE: The front entrance, wide enough for a horse and cart to go through. Watch for grooves in the wall where the portcullis slid up and down.

3) MURDER HOLES: Look for holes in the ceiling, especially as you come through the gatehouse. Also sometimes in the walls. Defenders could shoot arrows, drop rocks, boiling water or quicklime* on top of invaders.

4) THE KEEP: The part of the castle where people lived. It's usually a tall square or rectangular building near the middle of the castle.

5) FIREPLACES: A castle will have several of these, high up in the walls. The remnants of a chimney may still be there too.

6) JOIST HOLES: There will be many of these square holes in the walls where the timbers that held the floors were inserted.

* This was a substance that burned the skin.

7) SPIRAL STAIRS: Look for the remains of stairs that wind clockwise.

8) CHAPEL: Most castles had a chapel. You can tell where it was as there're usually finely crafted arched windows and a stone basin in the wall where holy water was kept.

9) ARROW LOOPS: Look for rectangular slits in the walls that widen as they go inward. This was so archers could fire their arrows at enemies in relative safety.

10) DUNGEON AND OUBLIETTE: Look for a deep hole in the ground where prisoners were kept. The oubliette was a tiny dungeon where prisoners were thrown into and forgotten about. ('Oubliette' comes from the French word *oublier* - 'to forget.') Don't fall in!

11) HOARD HOLES: Keep an eye out for rectangular holes on the outside castle walls. These supported beams that held wooden platforms called hoards which overhung the outside castle walls, making it easier for the castle's soldiers to defend it.

12) SALLY PORT: You can easily overlook this small back door about halfway up a wall where soldiers could 'sally forth', which means to leave the castle secretly.

13) WATERGATE: Some castles built near a river may have had a fortified gate that allowed supplies to be taken in by boat. Like the gatehouse, look for grooves in the wall where the portcullis slid up and down.

Remember always to have an adult with you when visiting a castle ruin. They can be dangerous places, even today!

NORMANS' LAND
LEGACY OF THE NORMANS

Apart from building castles all over the place, what else did the Normans do? Well, even while the castles were being constructed, villages would spring up around them, filled with workers and their families. Businesses thrived in these places because they met the everyday needs of the people who worked in and around the castle. Many of these villages grew into towns that still exist today.

The fact that you're reading this book means that the Normans did a good job of bringing the English language to Ireland. The Norman nobles mostly spoke French, but the ordinary settlers who came over from England spoke English, though we may not recognise it as English if we heard it today. A bit like when you visit your cousins up north or down south.

"BOUT YE, BIG LAD! YE GOIN' FER A WEE DANDER TE GET A POKE?"

* How are you, my good fellow? Would you like to come for a walk with me to buy some ice-cream?

Ireland is famous for its fertile green fields surrounded by stone walls or hedgerows. The Normans used a three-field system of crop rotation, with spring as well as autumn sowings. Wheat or rye was planted in one field, and oats, barley, peas, or beans were planted in the second field. Each year, the crops were rotated to leave one field fallow. It was the Normans who introduced this system as well as hay-making, which changed the nature of farming and food production in Ireland. They also started the process of making county boundaries, as Ireland had previously been divided into five provinces containing around 150 kingdoms.

The Normans gave us a lot of popular Irish surnames. See if your family name is among this lot:

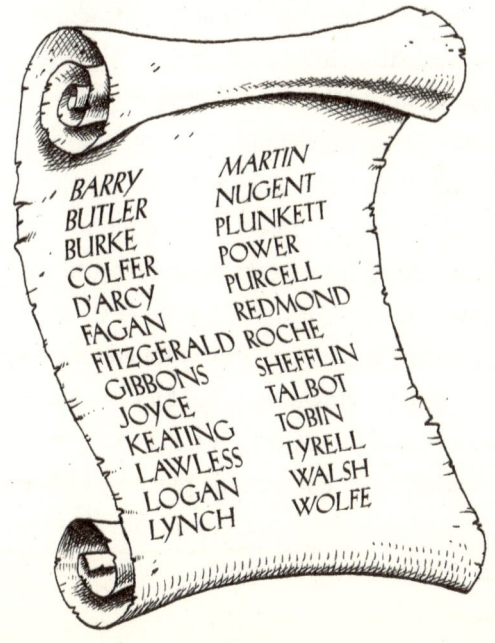

BARRY
BUTLER
BURKE
COLFER
D'ARCY
FAGAN
FITZGERALD
GIBBONS
JOYCE
KEATING
LAWLESS
LOGAN
LYNCH
MARTIN
NUGENT
PLUNKETT
POWER
PURCELL
REDMOND
ROCHE
SHEFFLIN
TALBOT
TOBIN
TYRELL
WALSH
WOLFE

Lots of the castles built in the Late Medieval Period are in ruins having been 'slighted' or partially destroyed in Oliver Cromwell's conquest of Ireland from 1649 to 1653. However, many are still standing and operate as hotels and tourist spots which you can go and visit yourself.

And it wasn't just castles the Normans were great at building. They used their knowledge of working with stone to construct beautiful churches, cathedrals, abbeys and monasteries. Many of these buildings are still in fine condition considering they are hundreds of years old. The Normans also founded many towns throughout the island of Ireland.

With connections all across Europe and Scandinavia, the Normans were responsible for developing bustling trade routes from Irish port towns. Already a thriving trade centre since Viking times, Dublin became the capital of Norman power in Ireland. They built strong defensive walls around the city that stretched north of the River Liffey and defined the streets. Although most of the wall is gone, some of the streets exist even today.

Thanks to the Normans, we have those long-eared, twitchy-nosed, big-footed, bushy-tailed, carrot-crunching cuties – *rabbits*! Nowadays, rabbits are kept mostly as pets. In medieval times they were an important source of food, skin and fur. For various reasons, their population has declined but there are still plenty of them hopping around every county in Ireland.

Loads of movies, TV shows, cartoons, games and events draw inspiration from the medieval era. Every so often, a new incarnation of Robin Hood comes along, proving how popular the imagery of medieval life is all across the globe. You can even dress up as a Norman knight or a jester or a wealthy noblewoman and go to one of the many renaissance fairs or medieval banquets held in and around castles.

So there was more to the nasty, naughty Normans than just a people who were invited to invade Ireland. Although they seized power and oppressed the native Irish, they did eventually fall under the Irish spell and become '*Níos Gaelaí ná na Gaeil féin*' – more Irish than the Irish themselves. There's no more **DEADLY!** legacy to echo down the hallowed halls of history than that!

FAMOUS IRISH CASTLES MAP

1) Athlone
2) Bagenal's
3) Ballygally
4) Birr
5) Blackrock
6) Blarney
7) Bunratty
8) Cahir
9) Carlingford
10) Carrickfergus
11) Cashel
12) Castle Roche
13) Clogh Oughter
14) Clonony
15) Dalkey
16) Donegal
17) Dublin
18) Dunguaire
19) Dunluce
20) Enniscorthy
21) Enniskillen
22) Ferns
23) Foulksrath
24) Greencastle
25) Huntington
26) Johnstown
27) Kilbrittain
28) Kilcoe
29) Kilkenny
30) King John's
31) Leap
32) Malahide
33) Narrow Water
34) Newtown
35) Rockfleet
36) Ross
37) Thoor Ballylee
38) Trim
39) Tully
40) White's

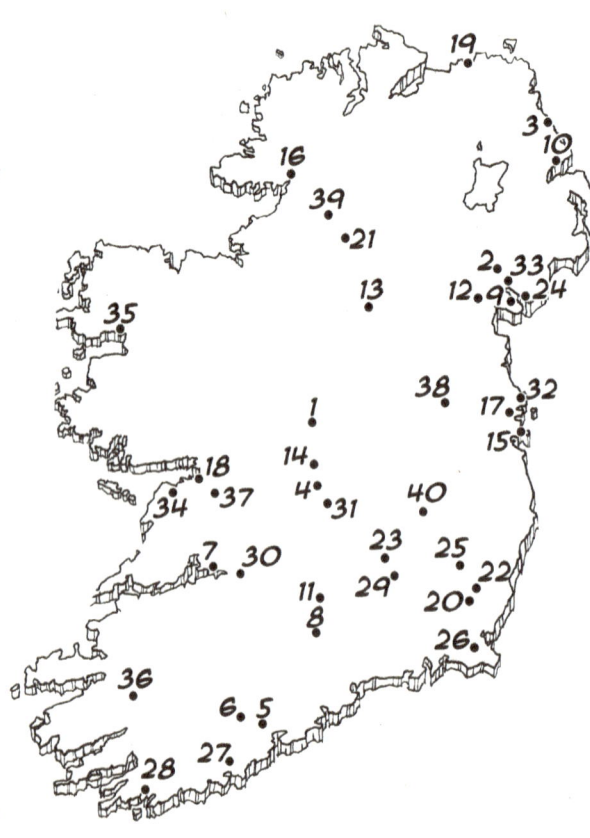

TIMELINE

911 – King Charles III (Charles the Simple) of France gives the Viking Rollo and his people a piece of the northern part of his kingdom (now called Normandy) in order to stop Rollo from pillaging the rest of France. The settlers become known as 'North Men' or 'Normans'.

1066 – Norman King William defeats English King Harold at the Battle of Hastings. William becomes king of England.

1070s-1080s – The Bayeux Tapestry is made in England, illustrating the Battle of Hastings. The Normans and Saxons of England begin to fuse together to become what historians call 'Anglo-Norman'. Those who settled in Wales were known as 'Cambro-Norman'.

1152 – King of Leinster, Diarmuid MacMurrough (Diarmait Mac Murchada) kidnaps Dervorgilla (Derbfhorgaill), the wife of Tiernan O'Rourke (Tigernán Ua Ruairc), King of Breifne.

1156 – Pope Adrian gives permission to Henry II of England to invade Ireland. That was nice of him! King Henry is so busy fighting other wars in France and elsewhere that the invasion of Ireland is not high on his list of priorities.

1167 – High King of Ireland, Rory O'Connor (Ruaidrí Ua Conchobair), takes the kingdom of Leinster from King Diarmuid MacMurrough for kidnapping Dervorgilla. This is what happens when you go around kidnapping other people's wives.

1169 – The first Normans arrive in Ireland after being invited by King Diarmuid MacMurrough who wants their help getting his kingdom back. In return, Diarmuid swears loyalty to King Henry II of England and promises Irish land to the Normans, even though it isn't his to give.

1170 – The Earl of Pembroke, Richard 'Strongbow' de Clare, lands in Ireland with 200 knights and 1,500 soldiers. King Diarmuid promises Strongbow his daughter Aoife's hand in marriage.

1171 – King Diarmuid dies. Strongbow claims the kingdom of Leinster for himself under Norman law despite Diarmuid's son, Domhnall, claiming the throne under the Irish Brehon law.

1171–72 – King Henry II visits Ireland and stays for six months. Concerned that Strongbow has too much land and power, he forces him to bow to his authority.

1170s – The Normans begin building temporary ringwork and wooden motte-and-bailey fortresses in strategic positions throughout Ireland. These take a short time to build and are meant to scare the bejapers out of the local population. It works, though a few Irish kings successfully burn some down.

1175 – The Treaty of Windsor is signed by Henry II and the last High King of Ireland, Rory O'Connor.

1176 – Strongbow dies of a leg infection.

1177 – Henry II authorises Norman lords to conquer more Irish land. He declares his nine-year-old son John to be 'Lord of Ireland'. Prince John doesn't visit Ireland for another eight years.

1178 – John de Courcy, a Norman knight, invades Ulster and begins building Carrickfergus Castle.

1180s – The first stone castles start to be built in Ireland, usually on the sites of motte-and-bailey fortresses. Most castles take between ten and twenty years to build.

1185 – Gerald of Wales is chosen to accompany King Henry II of England's son John on an expedition to Ireland. He writes two books about it, in which he doesn't have a lot of good things to say about the Irish. John de Courcy declares himself Prince of Ulster.

1189 – Henry II dies and is succeeded by his son Richard (Richard the Lionheart).

1315 – Robert the Bruce, King of Scotland, sends his younger brother Edward to invade Ireland.

1347 – The Black Death reaches Europe and spreads to Ireland the following year where it kills between 30 and 50% of the population. The wave of castle building stops until the 1400s.

1400s – Irish chieftains begin using Norman building techniques and start constructing their own tower house castles.

1500s – Due to new warfare technology such as gunpowder and cannons, castles are unable to withstand attack as well as they used to.

1640s – Oliver Cromwell leads the English armies in a wave of destruction and destroys many castles, leaving them in ruins.

ANSWERS TO DEADLY! MEDLEY (PAGES 30–31)

1. Well
2. Animal pens
3. Chickens
4. Storeroom
5. Meat and fish hung up
6. Moat
7. Drawbridge
10. Arrow loops
11. Spiral staircases
12. Cook
13. Hoard

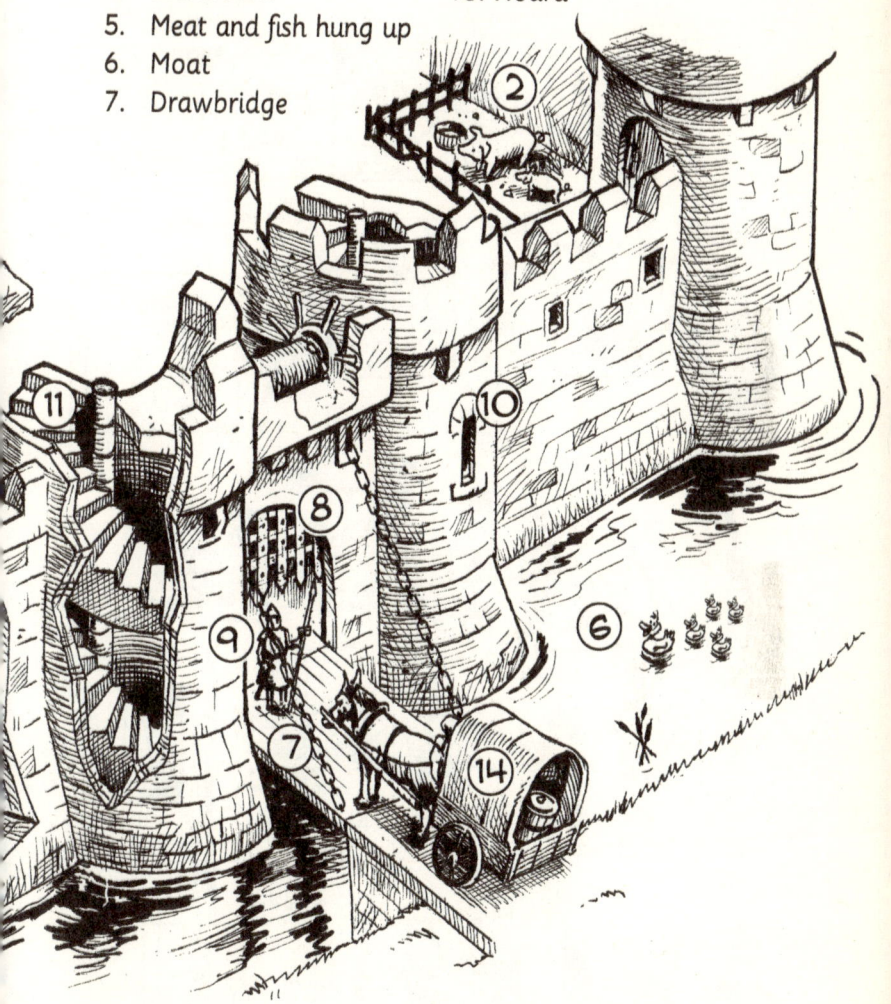

8. Portcullis
9. Gateman
14. Horse and cart delivering supplies

ANSWERS TO SÉAMUS THE SINISTER SWORDSMAN

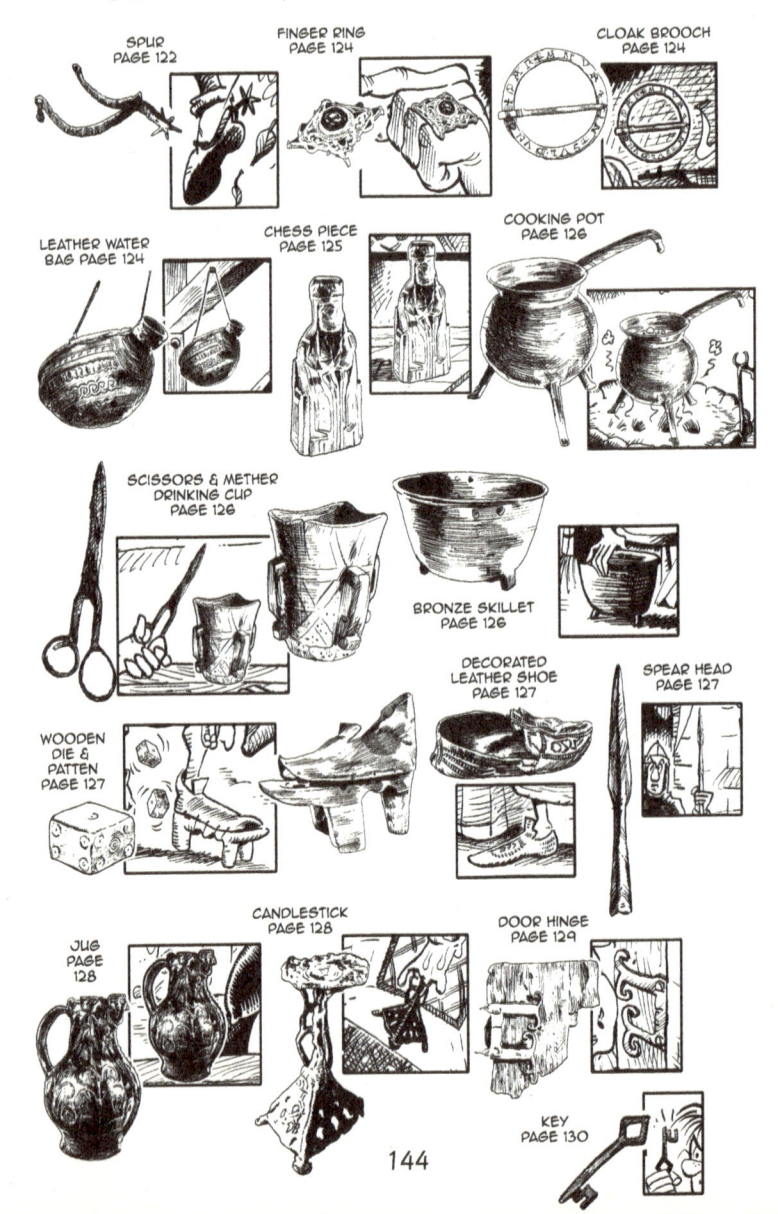

SPUR PAGE 122

FINGER RING PAGE 124

CLOAK BROOCH PAGE 124

LEATHER WATER BAG PAGE 124

CHESS PIECE PAGE 125

COOKING POT PAGE 126

SCISSORS & METHER DRINKING CUP PAGE 126

BRONZE SKILLET PAGE 126

DECORATED LEATHER SHOE PAGE 127

SPEAR HEAD PAGE 127

WOODEN DIE & PATTEN PAGE 127

JUG PAGE 128

CANDLESTICK PAGE 128

DOOR HINGE PAGE 129

KEY PAGE 130